The Guy who Returned Elvis' Ring

Frank Fernandez

BeachHouse Books, Chesterfield Missouri USA

The Guy Who Returned Elvis' Ring

Is copyright 2012 by Bernard Frank Fernandez.

All rights reserved

The cover photo of Elvis Presley was a promotional work obtained from Wikipedia.com, and assesed to be in the Public Domain, lettering and other enhancements by Robert J Banis, PhD

Paperback Edition (2012) ISBN-13: 9781596300811

Published 2012 by BeachHouse Books, an Imprint of Science & Humanities Press, Chesterfield Missouri USA

"LOOKING BACK, I'D HAVE TO SAY 'LIFE CAN BE INTERESTING' BUT THEN, IT WAS WHAT IT WAS."

Bernard (Frank) Fernandez

Stories

Elizabeth and Peter 1
Annie and Joe 6
The Fernandez "Roots" Odyssey 13
Millsboro – The Early Days 23
Steamboats on the Monongahela River 24
Then There was Jim and the Monongahela 25
Creative Little Boys 26
Herbert Seaton 27
High School Days and Three Notable Memories 29
Aunt Jenny 30
The Fantastic Fanfare 31
Max Findl 32
Highlights of My Army Air Force Service 33
Cherry Blossoms and a Night in Jail 37
University of Cincinnati 41
Three Calendar Years and a Minor Miracle 42
A Great Line 45
Three Jobs then a Big Decision 47
Alaska Airlines 48
The Day My Patience Ended 50
A Hilarious Example of Problem Solving 51

Fairbanks, Alaska 52
Commissioner of Baseball (in Fairbanks, Alaska)
.... 54
Come to the Fair 57
Two of Fairbanks More Interesting Characters .. 59
Woody 60
Sam Bowling – U. S. Marshall 62
An Old Neighbor in Fairbanks, Alaska 65
Interesting Insights into Alaska Airlines 66
The Beginning of the End 68
Airborne 69
My First "Shaker" 70
Mac 72
Turkey Eggs 75
Billy Barty and the Little People 81
Pacific Air Freight 83
The Second Mark IV 85
Doing Business in New York City 89
Max 91
The Tonight Show 94
The Teamsters 98
Raymond's Entrance Exam 99
The Polish Way of Pulling up Your Socks 100

Speaking Before the Teamsters	101
A Lesson Learned	102
In Defense of the U.S. Postal Service	104
Interesting Times in Europe	107
Dealing with Jet Lag	108
Santa Claus and the Easter Bunny	109
Fettuccini Alfredo	110
Dino and the Carbinieri	112
The Ups and Downs of Flying	114
The Little Boy on the Table	115
Two Unusual Flight Attendants	116
Stevie Wonder	119
Close Encounters of the Best Kind	121
Elvis and the Ring	122
Vince Lombardi	126
Dr. B	130
Charlton Heston	132
John Wayne	133
Stealing a Horse in Downtown Chicago	134
Empathy for Richard Nixon?	138
Notre Dame	140
Cary Grant and the Magic Castle	143
My Neighbor Leo	145

The Lady at the Tuck Box 147
Observations of a People Watcher 148
Gentleman A 150
Gentleman E 152
GOLF STORIES 155
Jack Nicklaus 156
The Marvelous Kiwis 166
Whoever Breaks a Window 168
Working as a Caddy 169
St. Andrews 171
Charles Hamm, Caddy Extraordinaire 172

****

Elizabeth and Peter

In 1909, my grandmother Elizabeth, her husband Peter and their 2-year-old daughter, Annie, arrived in America from Messina, Sicily. With a stopover in West Virginia, they settled in Millsboro, a very small town in the soft coal fields of southwestern Pennsylvania.

Peter was a nice, handsome man with a marvelous sense of humor and absolutely no ambition. When Elizabeth realized she would have to be the bread winner, she reacted with a dedication and a desire to succeed beyond anything one could imagine.

After Peter went to work in a coalmine, she started a small boardinghouse for coal miners. She also sold homemade wine. She later opened a grocery store. Although she could not speak, read or write English, she remembered every transaction until one of her children came home from school and recorded them in a journal.

In her relentless pursuit of money, she became a tyrant and engaged in behavior, that even with her children, was hard to believe. The most outrageous? Annie married young and became a mother in her teens. She and her husband and child lived in a small house owned by Elizabeth. Her own mother convinced Annie and her husband to burn their home to the ground for the insurance proceeds.

1

These proceeds would then be split between Annie and Elizabeth. It took two tries to get the job done!

My grandmother later explained to her daughter that the insurance payment was less than expected. She then told Annie to take her share in the form of items from the grocery store. So after Annie and Joe lost their home to a fire, they ended up in a little house down behind the local mortuary.

Peter continued to work in the coalmine. His reaction to the almost complete dominance by Elizabeth? Usually, on a Saturday evening, after a little too much wine, he would curse, in minute detail, every saint in the Catholic world. When he was through, he threatened Elizabeth with bodily harm. If she was crocheting, without looking up from her project, she would tell him to shut up and go to bed ending yet another of Peter's self-assertion sessions.

Two memories of Elizabeth are associated with the human gastro-intestinal area. The first was her inclination toward "eruptions". Just ONE could clear a room of family members within ten seconds. The only times I saw her laughing, almost hysterically, happened when she witnessed a small group of people trying to get through one door at the same time.

The second memory was of her providing a cure for such maladies as a garden variety stomachache. She would pour a small amount of olive oil into a saucer. She would then place the saucer over the bellybutton of the patient. The next step was drops of water falling into the olive oil while Elizabeth very softly gave forth a Sicilian chant. The cure rate? 100 percent. Who would dare tell the "doctor" they didn't feel better?

As a very young boy, I would describe myself as quiet, polite and almost shy. Having said that, and for reasons I've never understood, I was the only person in the family who wasn't intimidated by Elizabeth. She was always trying to frighten me by reciting the terrible things about to happen. My response? "You can't fool me you crazy old woman." She would then curse me in Sicilian, always accompanied by a smile.

After many years in Millsboro, Elizabeth moved her family to the suburbs of Philadelphia. She tried living on a small farm, but settled permanently in a nice home in Upper Darby. I believe the purchase was a cash transaction. In spite of her strong financial situation, Peter, well into his seventies, still came out of the front door dressed in his bib overalls and carrying his lunch bucket. He worked as a laborer for a construction company.

As expected, all of her children lived nearby. After being discharged from the Air Force, I stayed at my parents' home, also in Upper Darby, for about a year and joined my grandfather as a laborer.

It's easy to remember those days, particularly the trip, by car, to work. Peter's friend owned the car and I sat in the front seat between them. The smell of the smoke from their Sicilian cigars is still high in my memory bank.

Since we left at the same time every morning, we listened to the same radio programming. The owner never tuned in to any other station. So, we were privileged to listen to a Beneficial Finance commercial daily. Its content indicated that Beneficial's only reason for existence was to lend its customers as much money as they wanted at unbelievably low rates. At least two or three mornings every week, Peter would exhale a large amount of cigar smoke, then say "Porto la sacca" — Sicilian for "Bring a sack" to carry all the money they were going to give you. He knew it was a con.

My grandmother's public relations skills were in a class by themselves. Many years after the Air Force and college, my work involved a lot of time in New York City. As often as possible, I would drive down and say hello to my grandparents. I knocked on their screen door one lovely summer day and when Elizabeth saw it was me, she turned to Peter who was nearby in his rocking chair and said, "Peter, what was I telling you this morning?" He would shrug his shoulders with a look that said, "With all the things you tell me, how am I supposed to choose one?" Then "I was telling you my favorite grandson is Bernard!"

If my brother were to come by the next day, I guarantee she would go through the same routine.

After my grandmother's passing, her six children and six grandchildren experienced varying degrees of devastation. Those with the deepest feelings were puzzled because of her, shall we say, mixed record as a mother and grandmother. I offered the explanation that the strong difference between highs and lows didn't matter. Bottom line? She was a FORCE.

My personal reaction was to take a red-eye from Los Angeles to Philadelphia. I remembered a funeral scene from a movie The Godfather and bought enough red roses so each family member could place one on her casket.

Peter left some five years later.

Annie and Joe

My dear mother, Annie, arrived in America from Sicily at age two. She was the oldest and brightest of Elizabeth Perrone's six children. She was also the only one of the six who did not get a college degree. She left school after the sixth grade to help with her brothers and sisters and to work in my grandmother's boardinghouse. By work, I mean scrubbing floors and washing, by hand, the clothes of the boarders who worked in the coalmines.

My father, Joseph, one of the boarders, was a handsome young Spaniard recently arrived from the beautiful hills of northwestern Spain. Without one date, he and Annie ran away and were married. Two days later Annie called home and begged to return. Elizabeth's answer: "You made your bed now you must lie in it." Annie and Joseph's marriage remained strong until my father's passing at age seventy-eight.

I can't imagine a scenario where a human being could put forth a work effort as difficult as my father's in order to provide such a low standard of living for him and his family. His day began at 3:30 a.m. with a breakfast of coffee laced with wine and a piece of bread baked by my mother in the outside oven he built.

He then walked three miles to the coalmine where he shoveled coal, sometimes while standing in water. In winter, by the time he walked home in the sub-freezing temperatures of southwestern Pennsylvania, ice had formed on his pant legs.

It didn't take long for the mine environment to permanently damage his lungs. There were times when he couldn't make the short distance up a hill from the railroad tracks to our back gate. The breathing situation meant he had to sit up in a chair most nights.

In the seventeen years I lived in my father's house, I never heard him comment on how badly he felt or how tired or anything having to do with the negatives of his life.

While I clearly understood he was one of many immigrants who came to America in search of a better life, I can only speak to my father's situation since I witnessed it over a period of years.

The low standard of living referred to earlier translated into a heating system consisting of a small Hetrola (the manufacturer's name for a small stove) in our living room. In it we burned coal we were able to knock off the rims of the cars of the freight trains that passed a short distance from our house. You know your heating system is inadequate when you can see you breath INSIDE the house.

This low standard also meant an outhouse, no newspaper or telephone and wearing damp clothing to school. If there were dryers in those days I never saw one.

At some point in my late teens I began to engage in self-pity brought about by my living conditions. What followed next was my first serious encounter with logic and reason. I came to the conclusion that my mother and father, as parents, had done their very best. The rest of my life was up to me. I never again gave any serious thought to the negative aspect of my early years.

While financial pressures often cause marital problems, I heard harsh words between my mother and father just once. They were the result of Mom going to a house where Dad was playing cards with his friends. If you're interested in peace and tranquility you just don't do that with a proud Spaniard.

It wasn't long before my parents left Millsboro to join Elizabeth and Peter in the Philadelphia area. The important positive of this move was my father leaving the coalmines. He then became a bricklayer and stonemason.

Over a period of years, the condition of my father's lungs worsened. His doctors could only recommend a move to Arizona where the cleaner air might be a positive. Since they really had no choice, Mom and Dad moved to Phoenix. Fifty years ago, the air really was cleaner.

Initially, the change in location was a disaster. At one point, Dad's doctor told me to make funeral arrangements. Then, for reasons no one, including his doctor, could understand, he recovered and was with us for almost twenty years. I had witnessed a miraculous event.

I'll never forget my mother's words when we finally were faced with Dad's passing, "How can the sky be so blue and the sun so bright? He's going!"

Since our age difference was only fifteen years we were best friends as well as mother and son.

We seldom traveled together, but on this one occasion she was visiting her mother in the Philadelphia area at the same time I was working in New York City. We decided it would be an opportunity to spend some quality time together. I would drive down, pick her up and we would take a flight from JFK to Phoenix.

The departure day was a Sunday so I figured the traffic would allow us time for a leisurely trip from my Grandmother's house to the airport. Everything was going to plan until we reached midtown Manhattan where some emergency construction had resulted in a traffic situation.

It took some serious driving to get to the car rental office at JFK a short time before departure. There was no one in the rent-a-car office. I grabbed the designated phone on the counter, told the guy that answered about our time situation and asked if I could drop the car keys and paperwork into a slot beside the phone. A horrified voice pleaded, "Don't do that! The keys would seriously damage our computer." I followed his instructions and we walked through the plane's door just minutes before it was closed.

Though somewhat frazzled, I was proud of my efforts allowing us to make it. The fact this was a special fare flight for my mother and the next available would require her to overnight in New York just pushed up the pressure. After we were settled in our seats, from my mother: "Bernard, God doesn't want us to take this flight." From me, with considerable sincerity: "Then get the hell off!" She didn't and we had a nice, uneventful flight to Phoenix.

A considerable length of time after my father passed on, Mother began going to dances at a Senior Citizen Center. Her immediate popularity didn't surprise me. Our frequent phone conversations began to indicate a mutual interest between her and two gentlemen. One was a dancing partner and the other lived in the neighborhood. Sometime later it was apparent this interest had continued. One day I began our conversation by saying, "What's the latest on 'General Hospital' Mother?" She answered by saying the guy who lived nearby increased her pulse rate, but kept company with a lot of ladies and she didn't care to be one of them. The dancing partner Kenneth, some years her senior, wanted marriage, sooner rather than later."

I rarely give specific advice regarding relationships but this was my mother and it was also a no-brainer. "Mother, don't even think about marrying this guy. You gave

Dad the best nursing care for a long time — care that was very debilitating, both mentally and physically. At Kenneth's age you could be doing the same for him at any time. You've earned a decent life quality in your remaining years. While Kenneth's obviously a nice person, I think, even at his age, he's looking for another mother."

She took my advice, although she continued seeing him.

She lived in a modest two bedroom house and I visited her as often as possible and I always tried to keep it light when in her company. On this particular trip, she greeted me warmly and I responded by asking if she was running a first class hotel. I knew that Kenneth was staying there on weekends and I asked her if there was fresh bedding in the second bedroom. She almost blushed and said that Kenneth had been sleeping in her bedroom. I responded with a smile and, "Mother, you little rascal." This conversation took place at the front door. I didn't realize Kenneth was visiting when I arrived and was just around the corner.

Later in the evening my mother came into my room and said, "Bernard, Kenneth wants me to ask you a question."

"What?" I asked.

"He wants to know if he can stay here tonight."

Surprised wouldn't cover my reaction. Here was this strong, absolute queen of her domain asking her son such a question. My answer, "Mother, Kenneth stays overnight when I'm not here and I know it. Why should it be any different when I am here?"

In all the years of our relationship I had never experienced a similar feeling. I was absolutely charmed by the touch of innocence and her reverting to the mindset of a young girl.

The Fernandez "Roots" Odyssey

The idea of a "Roots" trip to Spain began on our annual Christmas visit to my mother and my brother and his family in Phoenix, Arizona. My sister-in-law, Jeanne, had suggested that my brother, Philip, and I make the trip to determine what part of our family might still be there. Our father had come to America at the age of nineteen and had never returned. Over the years his family had scattered to distant points and the correspondence between us was infrequent at best.

There had been some mention of Dad coming into possession of land but the primary reason as put forth by my dear sister-in-law was our version of "Roots". This struck an immediate chord with me. I had grown up with my mother's family close by but had never seen anyone related to my father.

Not unexpectedly, my brother decided against going. He was a very strong homebody, while I had begun traveling at age seventeen and never stopped until my later years.

On the return trip to our home in Pebble Beach we stopped over in Los Angeles to bring a little cheer to my wife Suzi's Mom. While reading the Los Angeles Times I saw an ad announcing Iberia Airlines' new non-stop service from Los Angeles to Madrid at a sensationally low fare. Additionally, I had given Suzi and IOU for a trip to Europe shortly before our wedding. We had initially planned to begin our marriage with a trip to Italy, France and Spain but had settled for Mauna Kea and other places in the Hawaiian Islands.

In other words, everything pointed to GO and the more I thought about it, the stronger the feeling became to go over and see if we could find anyone from my father's family. I was somewhat surprised at the strength of these feelings.

Two letters were sent to individuals believed to be my aunts, telling them about the upcoming visit. There was no specific knowledge that these individuals were in the country let alone in my father's birthplace, the village of Rios, Province of Orense.

It was no easy feat just to find Rios on a map. The California State Auto Association finally came forth with one in sufficient detail to find it with the help of the remembrance's provided by my father's description of the geographic location.

So, with no certainty that any members of the family were in Rios and unable to speak or understand the language, Suzi, our son Joseph and I departed on the 12th of April, 1987.

The "Happenings" before, during and after Rios should happen to every traveler in search of the trip of a lifetime.

In Madrid, the charming little hotel near the palace; the very professional and informative guide who took us through the Prado introducing us to the works, among others, of Velasquez, Goya, Murillo and El Greco. While I know very little about art, it was obvious these guys knew what they were doing; Then a walk through Retiro Park; followed by afternoon tea and goodies at the Ritz.

The departure from Madrid for Segovia will not soon be forgotten. We were fighting the clock because it was the afternoon of getaway day prior to Holy Week. After obtaining a little Opel from Avis, I started off with a bang by turning into what I thought was the hotel garage. It actually was a movie house and definitely not of the drive-in variety. This was clearly indicated by an agitated woman who was just trying to help.

After loading the car and warning Suzi and Joseph to prepare for possible whip lash, I engaged in a maneuver across several lanes of screaming traffic that got the attention of more than one Spanish driver. To achieve such a feat requires an act of daring so outrageous as to set a new standard for insanity. I felt it was necessary. The way to Segovia, had I turned the other way, was sufficiently confusing as to cause a delay of some consequence.

Upon our arrival in Segovia we parked near an ancient aqueduct and were accompanied to our hotel, a considerable distance away, by an elderly gentleman who wanted to be sure we didn't lose our way. We had only asked him for directions, but this is the kindness he showed us.

If there were more individuals in the Catholic Church like the priest who showed us through the cathedral in Segovia, I would have to consider a return to the Catholic faith. The moments spent with this man were magical. He exuded so much warmth, graciousness and style along with absolute simplicity we were left with renewed hope for our troubled world. Our visit ended with the priest bestowing a blessing on Joseph and he, the priest, in turn was more than a little startled by an enthusiastic hug from Suzi.

Our climb to the top of the Alcazar was invigorating and laughs were often and strong at dinner in the Duque Restaurant. Joseph tried to order lamb stew. The poor waiter almost wore a path in the wooden floor trying to get the right dish. His efforts were characterized by a look of sincerity, frustration and determination, all the while

maintaining, just barely, his composure. We didn't ever get what we consider lamb stew, but how could we tell him that?!

After leaving Segovia we found the "must see" castle in Coca where we met Francisco and family. Charming people with whom we traveled for some thirty hours. Our time together included a stay at the breath taking Parador in Leon which was an ancient monastery.

Suzi's camera was put to good use with subjects such as the windmills of Don Quixote. And then Rios.

Shortly after turning off the main highway at Benavente and heading toward Rios, the terrain changed from flat to gently rolling hills. In the distance were snowcapped mountains and as we got closer to Rios we reached elevations of 4,000 feet. Much of the ground was covered with purple flowers that looked and smelled, a little, like wild lilacs.

After passing through Pueblo Sanabria, which on the map appeared close to Rios, the nervousness and apprehension I had begun to experience once we were on our way to my father's birthplace, intensified. I had always taken pride in being in command of my emotions but I was experiencing unaccustomed levels and reacting sometimes too harshly to remarks from my wife and son. By this time it was late afternoon so looking for a very small town in an area where I had no perspective wasn't a plus for my mental state.

I decided to stop at a bar and ask for help. I looked at every one in the room and walked up to the person I thought to be the oldest. I gave this man the name of my grandfather, Don Bernardo Fernandez. He smiled and said, "Si." (Now mind you, prior to this event, we had traveled using Suzi's thirty or so words of Spanish. But I really felt

that this is where I needed to take over.) I then gave him the name of one of the Aunts we had written to in Rios and once again the man nodded, smiled and said, "Si."

17

It then occurred to me that this might be such a nice person he would nod agreement to any crazy American who wandered in from the highway and started mentioning names. So, the man named Manuel and I went to the other end of the bar and found a German woman who spoke some English and whose Spanish boyfriend knew some German. It turned out that the boyfriend's last name was Fernandez and he was a distant relative.

I spoke English to the woman who then spoke German to her boyfriend who spoke Spanish to Manuel. This process was then reversed. After a couple of minutes the woman indicated my family and I should follow her boyfriend's car.

Five minutes after leaving the bar, we were in the town of Rios. It was fortunate that I had stopped for information since the sign indicating Rios had been bent almost to the ground and would not have been easily seen.

Manuel led everyone to the house of Adelaide, my Aunt. She had our letter in her hand as she welcomed us warmly.

Manuel wandered off rather quickly but the woman and her boyfriend stayed for a considerable time and served as translators. After they left, Adelaide, Suzi, Joseph and I went to the house of Adelaide's son Eugenio. He and his family joined in a procession to the home of Candida, another Aunt whose lovely face so strongly resembled my father. She joined us and we proceeded to the house that was the birthplace of my father where we met Aurelia, the widow of my father's brother Manolo. If we thought the others were warm and loving, Aurelia took it to a new level.

I had never experienced a situation where I was unable to communicate with my own relatives. At the same time, as we walked from house to house, arm in arm, I had never felt closer to anyone.

Since it was Holy Week, another son of Adelaide, Julio, his wife Elena and their children were visiting. That evening after Paella and other goodies, Elena put on a special dress and danced the Flamenco as everyone clapped in unison.

Notwithstanding the difficulty of communicating we did learn my father was the youngest of thirteen children and was called "Pepe" by his family. My aunts spoke of my grandmother with reverence. She died at age sixty-three. Their feelings about my grandfather were not as positive.

The next day I went, alone, to the church of Rios some seventy-five yards from my aunt's house. I wanted to say a few words over my grandmother's grave. It was just to the left of the entrance. The church itself had fallen into disrepair but was still impressive because of its beautiful steeple. The front door was locked. Rios was so small, a priest came only on Sunday to conduct Mass.

As I stood a short distance from the church I remembered the words of my father describing Rios and the surrounding area. In the distance beyond the hills you could see Portugal. It was another perfect day. Apple trees in blossom and flowers everywhere. I could hear the sounds of doves and burros talked of by my father.

The beauty of the moment was accented when a precious little girl tugged on the leg of my pants then put her fingers to her lips in a "please be quiet" motion. She then ran down a pathway soon to be followed by her pursuing play mates.

The next morning, Eugenio came by with a Laurel tree that we planted in the front yard of my father's birthplace. A lovely memorial. I brought back one of the leaves for my brother and mine is framed and on a dresser in our bedroom.

Some months later when I was relating my time by the church to my mother, brother and sister-in-law, I amazed them and myself by bursting into tears. They didn't know what to do and finally my sister-in-law walked over and put her arms around me and offered that my father really was so very special. They didn't understand that I wasn't crying over my father's death. I was crying because of my father's life. Having come from the idyllic Rios to the land of opportunity where he worked like an animal in the coalmines, lost his health and only because of a strength beyond description, survived into his seventies. Some life.

When we left Rios I had such a strong feeling of pride that I was related to these people. Candida with her dazzling smile and gracious manner.

Adelaide much more austere, but so loving. Both with a dignity and a lot more than a touch of class. All of them so giving and just plain nice.

I was particularly touched when Adelaide later responded to my letter by telling me how much she enjoyed our visit and that she prayed I would return because she had so many things to tell me. I had promised shortly before leaving Rios, that I would return as soon as possible and when I did I would communicate in Spanish!

I intended to keep those promises but shortly after returning to Pebble Beach our home and everything in it was destroyed by fire. That was the main reason I didn't follow through on either promise.

After leaving Rios we stayed in Salamanca for one night then drove to Seville where we overnighted with the parents of Adelaide's daughter-in-law, Elena. Their warmth and hospitality were an exact continuation of our experience in Rios.

From Seville we proceeded along the Costa del Sol to Marbella and Torremolinos. We then turned toward Madrid visiting Granada, Cordoba and Toledo along the way. Our most memorable overnight was a castle where our room seemed suspended in air some 3,000 feet above the village of Jaen.

The visual beauty throughout the trip was such that one began to suffer from overload: Cathedrals, castles, sheepherders tending their flocks, cities that only needed borders to become breathtaking paintings.

The weather was perfect. A lot of blue sky accented with very white clouds and temperatures in the high sixties and low seventies. The Madrid-Los Angeles flight was smooth and uneventful with much time for reflection.

Millsboro – The Early Days

I was born in the tiny town of Millsboro, Pennsylvania located on the western bank of the Monongahela River some forty miles from Pittsburgh. When my contemporaries and I weren't in school and depending on the time of year, baseball, basketball and football plus hiking in the nearby forest was about it.

Once in a while there would be a little trouble. In those days trouble could mean something terrible like stealing a case of soft drinks from the delivery truck. When this actually happened, the authorities quickly swung into action. I should say authority since one man was the law for the area.

With his years of experience he knew that any chain was only as strong as its weakest link so he chose Davey Hanna to be the focus of his investigation. Davey was a decent kid who could never be described as the brightest bulb on the tree. It didn't come as any great surprise then when Davey cracked under the merciless interrogation he was undergoing and blurted out, "You think I'm gonna tell on my own cousin?"

Steamboats on the Monongahela River

Steamboats propelled by their large paddlewheels going up and down the Monongahela River are a sight to behold. They provided the power to push large barges used to transport coal.

As a young boy, I didn't understand why the barges looked so different depending on whether they were going up river or down river. In one direction almost all of their structure was above water. In the other direction they were 90 percent submerged.

Do you think the difference was caused by their being empty going up river and full of coal going down river?

Happily, I didn't mention my puzzlement to my parents. They would have put me in a place for the mentally impaired.

Then There was Jim and the Monongahela

Even a tiny place such as Millsboro had a swinging man-about-town bachelor who escorted pretty women and drove flashy cars.

We'll call him Jim. As indicated earlier, Millsboro was located on the western bank of the Monongahela River. Even though it was at minimum a half-mile wide, a cold winter created ice so thick a truck loaded with coal could drive from shore to shore.

A frozen surface of this size presented a marvelous opportunity for any daredevil that could get hold of a set of wheels, get it going as fast as possible, and then hit the brakes.

Naturally, the pacesetter and center of attention was Jim. This one winter he could hardly wait to get out there since he had just purchased a new Hudson Terraplane convertible.

When it happened, it wasn't gradual. Jim had separated himself from the rest of the vehicles and had motored down near a bend in the river. One second his new car was completely visible, the next second it hit some thin ice and disappeared. Happily, Jim was rescued. The car? Dead on arrival when it was finally pulled to shore.

Creative Little Boys

Once little boys learn to wet, they can become very creative. Many of us have heard of artistic efforts in the snow.

For some reason the chicken coop in my Grandmother's backyard had escaped my attention. I decided to correct this omission. The coop and a sizable open area were surrounded by a wire fence. It was the type of fence that provided several openings, which allowed me to accomplish my objective of going inside the pen without actually entering.

I had just completed my mission when a curious, LARGE, rooster wandered over, checked things out, and decided it looked enough like a worm, albeit a small one, to give it a go. It took a long time to get over that one.

Herbert Seaton

Herbert was a childhood friend. He was a very important person to all the kids that participated in sports. Herbert's father was our town's only dentist thereby enabling Herbert to own a lot of athletic equipment. Without this equipment, our baseball and football teams would have been primitive at best. No one else in our group had access to even small amounts of money.

Herbert was also fun to watch, particularly when he played the position of pitcher in our baseball games. His body seemed to be made up of sharp angles and when he let loose of the ball, his eyes had a peculiar look. When I was at bat against him I had a hard time concentrating on the ball's location.

After high school I knew he enrolled at Penn State, but years went by before I saw him at a University of Pittsburgh-Penn State football game. I was delighted but not surprised to learn that he had become one of the youngest assistant professors ever. The Pitt-Penn State rivalry was well-known for what happened after the game. The winning team wanted to take down the goal posts and the losing team engaged in serious disagreement.

At this particular game, Penn State won so their people wanted those goal posts down. I was a non-combatant but I hung around to witness this second contest. The last time I saw Herbert, the arms and legs of his gangly frame were wrapped around a goal post crossbar.

When talking to Herbert before the game I took notice of his expensive gabardine top coat. It was then stylish to have a slash in the back from the hem upward for ten or twelve inches. Because of his position on the crossbar, Herbert's coat was hanging straight down. Someone reached up, took hold of each side of that slash and tore it right to Herbert's neck. He then disappeared into a large, very active group of people!

High School Days and Three Notable Memories

Aunt Jenny

Eleventh Grade English was administered by my Aunt Jenny. She knew I was a daydreamer and tried to catch me off guard with a quick question. Her efforts were wasted since I always tuned in enough to answer quickly and correctly.

This ongoing game may have caused some frustration. That, plus some rather small activity that I can't remember, prompted her one day to send me to the principal's office.

More out of mischief than malice I went over to my grandmother's that evening and recounted her daughter's actions. Jenny received a severe tongue lashing a la "How do you expect this poor boy to learn if you throw him out of your class?"

The Fantastic Fanfare

Among the musicians in our high school band were four sensational trumpet players that should be mentioned by name: Jimmy Bartoletti, Aldo Battistoli, Joseph Mazeppa and Martin Costa. Jimmy was on his way to becoming a composer so he wrote a fanfare for four trumpets that was unbelievable (and I don't use superlatives that often).

As Student Conductor of the Band, I had to make a plea for funds at the annual spring concert. His fanfare blew the roof off the auditorium just prior to my appearing from behind the stage curtain.

No one's appearance could justify that fanfare so I did the only thing I could do, I showed my head and laughed. The audience joined in the laughter and my announcement was off to a good start.

Max Findl

Max Findl owned a grocery store about one mile from our house. My friendship with his son was a positive in Max giving me a job working Saturdays.

Max could have played an important role in Fiddler On The Roof without changing his appearance in any way ... brown fedora worn toward the back of his head, constant cigar, mustache, big belly covered by an apron that looked a little the worse for wear and black shoes up to his ankles with the laces always untied.

No matter how many times Max came into proximity to me on those Saturdays, he'd ask me the same question, "Tink you ever amount to any tink?"

The highlight of my work day was the arrival of the fresh baked goods. I would literally consume most if not all of a cherry pie every Saturday morning.

This one morning I was somewhat disappointed at the toughness and taste of the crust. I had eaten about one quarter of the pie before I realized I hadn't removed the cardboard underneath.

Highlights of My Army Air Force Service

I enlisted in the Army Air Force when I was seventeen. I thought flying an airplane would be cool and I liked the uniform. By the time I began active duty, World War II was winding down and the need for flight personnel was dwindling. I went through basic training a couple of times then to a school dealing with sheet metal and finally settled in a separation center. I hadn't a clue on a discharge date. In that time frame they were using a point system to determine when we could return to civilian life. Participating in combat meant you had a lot of points. Since I had been fortunate and not seen any combat I didn't have many points.

Then we were offered a deal where we could transfer from the Army of the U.S. to the regular Army, serve one year less thirty days terminal leave and that would be it. And we would be stationed in Europe — heady stuff for a young man from Millsboro, Pennsylvania. My good friend Herbert (Utts not Seaton) and I quickly accepted.

After a short leave we began our new adventure by hitchhiking from Pennsylvania to North Carolina. It's easy to remember that trip. One of our rides was courtesy of two guys from Brooklyn, New York. While driving late at night somewhere in the Carolinas, we unfortunately ran over a possum or a raccoon, I couldn't be sure. The driver was mortified and yelled, "My gawd! We've killed a pig."

The stay in North Carolina was short. Our orders had been changed and our new destination was Salt Lake City, Utah. So much for Europe, but ever optimistic Fernandez is thinking: The South Pacific wouldn't be too bad. From Salt Lake City, we moved to Seattle, Washington, still a logical point of departure for the South Pacific. Then the

never forgotten words: "Fernandez, Bernard; Adak, Aleutian Islands." For those of you not familiar with the location of Adak, there is a necklace of islands extending from the state of Alaska out into the Bering Sea, one of the most turbulent bodies of water in the world. Adak is close to the middle of this necklace.

Our troop ship left Seattle at midnight. I was too excited to sleep. Even though the S.S. Carl Schurz was only 25,000 tons, it was humongous compared to the steamboats I used to watch on the Monongahela River.

About 4 a.m. I said to one of the crew: "I guess we're really out in it," meaning the Pacific Ocean. His answer, "Relax sonny, we won't be out of the sound until this afternoon." I finally went to sleep.

When I was awakened at 6 a.m. for duty in the mess hall, I took one step, paused, and then headed for the latrine, a term used in the military meaning restroom. I spent most of the next three days and nights in that area. For the first and only time in my

34

life, I didn't care about living. I was that sick. I didn't even care when I heard the crew talking about a pool they had going. The ship was way past its retirement and they were betting on the date it would break up.

When we finally docked at our first stop, Dutch Harbor, my uniform hung rather loosely. As I was getting used to walking on land, I saw a guy fishing. Upon closer observation, I realized this would be my first meeting with an Eskimo so I'm trying to decide my method of communication. Not to worry. This guy had been a crewmember on a U.S. Air Force bomber and had flown 38 missions over Germany. His English was, at minimum, as good as mine.

We completed our debarkation at Adak in a driving rain. On a nearby roof, I saw three huddled soldiers trying their best to effect repairs. As we were going through our initial processing, I was asked if I could type. Remembering those guys on the roof my answer was immediate and strong, "Sergeant, you won't believe what I can do with a typewriter."

Actually, I ended up in charge of the Alaskan Air Command Aircraft Status Board. It was a fairly simple job but my "report to" didn't know anything about its operation. We agreed to the following deal: I guaranteed he would never have the slightest problem with that board. In return he would allow me reasonable freedom of movement. For example: If I had been up all night playing poker, I could nap for a couple of hours in the medic's area. We got along so well I received a promotion.

Happily, I had no problem dealing with the disappointment of Adak instead of Europe. I did my job, won a few bucks playing poker, and played a lot of basketball.

My ongoing loyalty to Notre Dame football could have gotten me into trouble. I was listening to the Notre Dame-Army game, one of the greatest in their long and storied history. The radio reception was bad. It was a critical part of the game, and the people behind me were talking, loudly. So without looking to see who was making all the noise, I yelled, "For God's sake will you guys shut up?" The "guys" were a general, a colonel, and a major. Fortunately, they were men of good humor.

While I wasn't looking forward to the sea voyage back to the States, my discomfort factor was tolerable and I finally received my discharge in New Jersey.

Cherry Blossoms and a Night in Jail

While I was in the Air Force, my family moved from Millsboro, Pennsylvania to a suburb of Philadelphia. Happily this relocation took my dad out of the coalmines into the fields of bricklaying and stonemasonry.

I was watching a movie in the local theatre on a Sunday afternoon when my brother came in and asked if I'd like to join him and a couple of his friends on a trip to see the cherry blossoms in Washington, D.C. The movie wasn't that interesting and I had never visited that area so in a short while we were on our way.

The blossoms were beautiful and after a brief stay we headed home. With just a few miles to go we ran out of gas. Ironically this happened in front of a gas station that was closed for the night.

A short time later a car came by and the driver said he was going near our house and had room for two. We decided my brother and one of his friends should take advantage of the kind offer while our car's owner, Joe, and I tried to solve our problem.

While I was checking the unlocked gas lines, Joe was examining the possibilities on the side and back of the station. My efforts were unsuccessful, but Joe found a truck with a plug in its accessible gas tank. He was able to loosen it and the result was a small flow of gas creating rivulets in the surrounding dirt.

37

As we were trying to find a container, another car came into the immediate area with colors and markings indicating that it was an Upper Darby police car.

I went over to the driver's side and explained our problem. The officer was quite pleasant and said he would be happy to take us home. Just about then, Joe came around

the corner of the station. As soon as the Policeman recognized Joe, his demeanor changed, dramatically. He quickly exited his vehicle, yelled in Joe's direction, "You!" Then ordered both of us to place our hands against the car and spread our legs. After patting us down, he ordered us into the police car and took us in.

The reason for the officer's sudden change of attitude? The previous Fourth of July, this particular cop was in his mobile unit peacefully dozing in the noon day sun. Joe had purchased a large quantity of the most violent fireworks he could find, placed them under the unit and set them off. It must have sounded like the beginning of World War III.

You can imagine this gentleman's reaction. A mild concussion from his head bounding off the car's ceiling, wetting his trousers and significant bruises from trying to exit are definite possibilities.

Joe was the prime suspect since he was a known prankster, but the police could never prove it.

I made my allotted phone call, my brother answered. When I told him I wouldn't be home because I was in Jail he repeated the word "Jail" so loudly my mother couldn't help but hear it. Motherly exclamations followed.

Joe and I were released the next morning since they couldn't come up with any charges that would keep us there.

From my viewpoint, two negatives: I had recently purchased an expensive camel's hair topcoat with part of my poker winnings while on Adak. Since there was no bedding in my cell I rolled it up and used it as a pillow. Finally, after returning home, I had to listen to my mother's admonitions. Her main, oft repeated offering? "My own

son, a common criminal. The neighbors will take their children into the house when they see you coming!"

I should have watched the movie.

University of Cincinnati

Three Calendar Years and a Minor Miracle

After completing my military service I enrolled at the University of Cincinnati and three calendar years later, aided by a minor miracle, I graduated with a Bachelor of Science in Education.

I say minor miracle because I carried a full load, 18 units, while working up to thirty- five hours per week.

Barely hanging on grade- wise, I was finally told by my faculty advisor that I needed a B grade in an upcoming literature exam to stay in school and graduate.

One of my worst defects is a lack of discipline. It was perfectly logical then to arrive the evening before this critical test almost totally unprepared. I then devised a brilliant plan. After work, come straight back to my room, study all night and go right to the 8:00 a.m. exam.

I had to make one transfer on the trolley line I used to and from work. It was a balmy evening so I decided to walk to the next stop rather than wait where I got off. This neighborhood was not exactly uptown — dishwater came cascading down from a third story window, etc.

I started to pass the entrance to what I'll kindly call a saloon when I heard music. It sounded live and the piano was right in there with the well-

42

known jazz pianists of that time. Without hesitation I went in. None of the people who lined the bar looked like they even heard the music.

In the very back I could see a small figure hunched over the piano. He was accompanied by drums and a bass fiddle.

I took a seat near the group. After the first break I approached the piano player, complimented him on his artistry and then diplomatically asked why he had chosen this particular venue to perform. He said that he had recently graduated from the Miami University of Ohio School of Music and that he was almost totally blind and this was the best he could do. Then, heartbreakingly, he looked up at me and said he believed the clientele was improving.

I stayed until closing.

It must have been about 3:30 or 4:00 a.m. before I started to scribble some notes on the morning's test. The next thing I knew I awakened with a meaningless scrawl ending my note taking. It was 7:30 a.m. I threw some water on my face and barely made it to the classroom with a few minutes to spare.

When I opened the Blue Book, I saw that it was a one question exam: Make comparisons among the different poets we had studied using passages from their poems.

I actually started to write the words 'Thank you and goodbye,' then paused and thought: Hell, if I'm

43

going to go down I might as well make it a flaming exit.

Here's a small sampling of my answer:

T. S. Eliot: I not only didn't have a clue about what he was saying, I didn't understand the notes on the side of the pages, which I guess were supposed to help you understand.

Ezra Pound: They never should have let him leave the loony bin.

I did say positive things about Robert Frost and Carl Sandburg.

When I received the test results there was a B Grade and the words "quite original" beneath it.

A Great Line

My political science professor was an interesting man. One of his close friends was the Prime Minister of Australia. He referred to their friendship on so many occasions we had a pool going. The winner would guess the number of times he would mention this relationship in the time frame of a semester.

One of the best lines I've ever heard came from a quick-witted fellow student. Punctuality was extremely important to this political science professor. The class room door was closed at 9:00 a.m. exactly. If you opened that door at 9:01 your grade took a hit.

Then came THE day. At 9:03 our professor had not arrived. Absolute silence from some thirty students. Then, from Quick -Witted, "Somebody close the door and he'll think he's already in here."

I borrowed the money to pay for my diploma and my dear mother made a present of my class ring on my next birthday.

Three Jobs then a Big Decision

Alaska Airlines

My first full time job was with Alaska Airlines in Seattle, Washington. Alaska was just beginning service originating in Portland, Oregon stopping in Seattle then flying non-stop to Fairbanks in what was then The Territory of Alaska.

After a short interview, two guys and I became responsible for all the functions of the cargo department in the airline's most important station. Our collective experience in air cargo was zero.

One of the guys, let's call him Al, did a good sales job on our supervisor, named Dick, and was placed in charge of me and the other guy. That arrangement changed in two weeks. Al was last seen heading for Vancouver, B. C. accompanied by a case of Scotch.

In that two week time frame, the other guy, we'll call him Percy was working on Dick so he was then placed in charge of me.

A short time later, and I have no idea why I remember this, someone in shipping from a company named Lentz Plumbing and Heating out of Bremerton, Washington called in a pickup. The answer he received? "Got a fire going, call you back." It seems Percy also had a booze problem, had fallen asleep at his desk and dropped his cigarette into a waste basket. This caused considerable excitement at Sea-Tac Airport.

That same day, Dick called me into his office and told me I was now in charge ...

of myself?

My exact response, "Dick, you son-of-a-bitch, I really appreciate the confidence you're showing in me."

We did some hiring and before long I was in charge of four individuals.

The owner of our company, R. W., was an eccentric multi-zillionaire from New York. His clothes were brightly colored; he drove a Lincoln convertible (almost always with the top down), and wore a hearing aid that never seemed to function when salary increases were being discussed. His interest in acquiring more and more money reached ridiculous levels.

If he was holding a short term investment in which the monies were not due for three to five days after the employees were to receive their paychecks, too bad for the employees.

The people I supervised were decent, hardworking, and living from paycheck to paycheck.

I quickly tired of hearing their polite but sad tales of woe regarding the effect our leader's irresponsible behavior had on their lives.

The Day My Patience Ended

In that time frame, practically everything that would fit into an airplane was flown to Alaska. The Alcan Highway was yet to be developed where it could accommodate regular truck traffic.

For Seattle, it was a particularly warm summer day and there were several thousand pounds of freight, much of it perishable, set up for movement to Fairbanks, Alaska. I went into Dick's office and told him that freight wasn't going anywhere until the cargo department's employees' checks were, not promised, but in their hands. Dick told me I would almost certainly lose my job, but he would inform the people in charge of my ultimatum.

We were the only department in the station to quickly receive our checks. The freight moved and for reasons that Dick never understood. I wasn't fired.

A Hilarious Example of Problem Solving

On a much lighter note ... I knew this truck driver who worked for a freight company that used Alaska Airline's service. When Jim was driving his vehicle he was ultra-careful. Put him behind the wheel of one of his employer's trucks and he became a man possessed.

One night he was running late for the Alaska flight AND he was hauling an interesting load of freight. Among other items were two or three live goats and some quarters of fresh beef. A goodly amount of the pee that Jim's driving scared out of the goats happened to land on the beef. Jim knew the airline people wouldn't accept beef with the strong odor caused by the frightened goats. Soooo, before delivering to the airline, he sprayed the beef with some strong cologne he had hastily obtained from one of the airport's shops.

I'm sure our cargo people wondered about the exotic smelling beef, but all of Jim's freight did move.

Fairbanks, Alaska

After supervising the Cargo Department for a matter of months, a new V.P. of Sales came on board and convinced me I could become a decent salesman. I worked in sales throughout the state of Washington, did pretty well and was promoted to the Sales Manager's job in Fairbanks, Alaska.

After settling in, I understood the enormity of the challenge I faced. Our main competitor was Pan American, at the time one of the world's largest airlines. We might have been the smallest. Both airlines flew the same type of aircraft and the fares were also the same. My take on the situation said that potential passengers would favor Pan American. They would figure that a large airline would have more resources, such as money, to maintain their aircraft and that they would have pilots with more experience than a small airline just starting.

There wasn't much I could do from a direct sales viewpoint. The single travel agency in town leaned toward Pan American. Alaska's destinations were limited while Pan Am's were worldwide.

Selling Alaska's freight service was a possibility but the entire area could be covered in a short period of time. Also, passenger traffic was by far the best source of revenue. So, I decided to take a personal approach. I would become involved in every civic activity that would place me in a favorable light with the entire population of Fairbanks.

Commissioner of Baseball (in Fairbanks, Alaska)

My first project involved my election to run the corporation that administered baseball on all levels, from Little League to the men.

When I met with the Board of Directors I told them my first priority was a new ballpark. Snickers and whispers greeted my announcement. My response, "I know you folks have heard that song before but this is a different ballgame, so to speak. If you check tomorrow's newspaper you'll see I've issued a call for volunteers to tear down what the people in town refer to, usually with a laugh, as our present ballpark. We'll either have a decent facility by opening day or there will be no baseball in Fairbanks this summer. It's a minor miracle there haven't been some serious injuries. I've never seen a situation where the sun sets over the center field fence for the men's games. I sure as hell wouldn't want to be a batter facing a pitcher with good stuff and lousy control. Any questions or comments?" Silence. End of meeting.

The demolition was going well until I was introduced to this guy who had arrived in a pickup truck. He said, "I don't know you but I'm for anyone who's trying to help the kids. What can I do for you?"

I told him I appreciated his offer and pointed to a section of the stands we hadn't been able to move,

"Can you get that section out of there?" "I'll do it," he said.

He backed his truck to a point a few feet away from the area I had indicated. He then took a long length of chain from the bed of his truck, wrapped one end around the rear axle and the other end around the bottom of the section we had been unable to move.

After revving his engine to a high level he popped the clutch. The truck shot forward and so did that piece of stand. Unfortunately, we didn't realize there was a guy-

wire attached to that piece. This guy-wire was an important support for a high metal chimney rising from a laundry right behind the stands. When the guy-wire snapped, that chimney started to sway. There were several people working in the laundry. It must have come within a couple of inches of falling.

I'll never forget the response to our project. Suppliers sold us materials at their cost. Carpenters waiting for work offered their services in exchange for a free dinner. A heavy equipment operator loaned us his D-8 Cat, a big and efficient earth mover, for several days, FREE and on, and on, and on.

At 3:30 a.m. on Memorial Day, the beginning of Baseball Season in Fairbanks, we were putting up three large pieces of camouflage netting that became our backstop. Our ballpark was complete and all levels of baseball, Little League, Pony League and the men enjoyed successful seasons.

Most of the baseball programs annual revenues came from one event, the Midnight Sun Game. It was held on the 21st of June and to the best of my knowledge was the only baseball game in the world that began at 11:30 p.m. without the aid of artificial light. Since June 21st is the longest day of the year and with Fairbanks being that far north, the sun really doesn't set. People who had no interest in baseball lined up for that one, just to say they'd been there.

Come to the Fair

When the wheels in Fairbanks realized they had a live one, they came after me for other projects. I became the Manager of the Tanana Valley Fair.

I had checked with my boss and he gave me the green light. He noticed that passenger traffic out of Fairbanks was increasing.

I should note here that I had forgotten my initial motivation for getting into the civic swing of things. I don't think anyone would argue with the fact that it's gratifying to witness the positive effect one's actions has on the lives of other people. This takes on another dimension for someone still in their twenties.

I knew absolutely nothing about running a Fair. As if that wasn't enough, the people that gave me the job had high hopes I could erase the red ink that had accumulated over a period of years.

It's not easy coming up with an attraction that would set new attendance records for a fair. Thank goodness for a guy named Johnny Albright, the owner of Fairbanks Plumbing and Heating. I asked him if he had any ideas. He responded by saying "How about a rodeo?" VOILA!

We brought in about twenty wild horses from the Peace River country in Canada.

Once we had them in the corral we had constructed I learned that we had a lot of self-proclaimed bronco busters in Fairbanks. One of them didn't even get the EE out of yippee before he was flying through the air. There was a waiting list of battered and bruised guys for the ambulance that would take them to the local hospital.

Johnny's assistance in putting on this Rodeo couldn't be measured and as you might imagine we were really pumped on opening day.

THEN we discovered that a highway contractor, for reasons only he knew, decided to do some work on the only road leading to the fairgrounds.

As Johnny's pickup approached the area where the number one guy was working, we were stopped by a young man. Before he could say anything, Johnny quietly said, "Son, you get two choices. You can let us through or you can stand there and get run over. Makes no difference to me." The young man moved, we found number one and all of the work came to a screeching halt shortly thereafter.

The people did 'Come to the fair' and we came within a whisker of wiping out the accumulated debt.

In addition to the Rodeo we of course had what you would expect at a fair, prize livestock, produce, etc., etc.

Two of Fairbanks More Interesting Characters

Woody

There were a lot of privately owned small aircraft in Fairbanks since there was no other way to get to the numerous outlying villages. Woody, the owner of a sleek, four-passenger plane asked one bright, sunny day if I would like to join him on a trip to one of these villages. He was transporting a young mother and her baby to a place called Chicken. I thought it would be a nice way to get an up close view of the surrounding countryside. About half way to our destination Woody said, "Hey Fernandez, you ever seen a moose?" I answered in the negative where upon Woody made a sharp turn and descended so rapidly the woman started to scream and the baby joined her. When Woody pulled up we seemed to be ten feet from a startled moose that had been feeding in a small stream. The rest of the trip was uneventful.

About a week later I saw Woody on Fairbanks' main street and he asked if I would do him a favor. "What's the favor Woody?" I asked.

"I have to deliver a message to a couple of guys who are camped out on a river bank down by Big Delta."

"What's the big deal about you throwing it out the window when you go by?"

60

"Well, they're in a canyon and I'll have about three or four feet tolerance on each side of my wing so I'll have to concentrate on flying that thing."

"See you around Woody."

Sam Bowling – U. S. Marshall

Between my community activities and guys like Woody, life in Fairbanks was seldom dull. Unfortunately, the same couldn't be said for a large number of the people living in Fairbanks.

Almost every Sunday afternoon a substantial group of local citizens would be at the airport. They just wanted to watch the takeoff of two commercial flights.

Our chief law enforcement official was a character named Sam Bowling. U. S. Marshal Sam Bowling to be exact. Sam really didn't have a lot to do but he certainly enjoyed acting like his version of a U. S. Marshal. For example; Sam knew when the last commercial flight left on Sunday. He would then position himself on the only road leading back to town with his speed set exactly on the speed limit. Everyone knew Sam and therefore knew the drill. No one would dare pass him.

Then along came Jim (he of the goats, beef and cologne). He had been recently transferred to Fairbanks and still was the Barney Oldfield of truck drivers.

On this particular Sunday afternoon he was running late with a load of freight that had to be in town ASAP. When he saw this long line of cars moving, by his standards ever so slowly, there was only one course of action.

When Jim zoomed past the first car in line, Sam couldn't believe his good fortune. He turned on his red light, pulled Jim over and wrote the ticket.

Of course, Jim asked me to intervene. Sam and I were friends since he was the Manager of a Little League team. After I approached him on the matter he never mentioned safety … he just said, "Damn it Frank, he can't do that. I'm the U. S. Marshal." Sam finally did relent.

When I dropped by Sam's office one day he couldn't wait to show me his latest toy. It looked like a fountain pen.

"See this Frankie boy. Think it's a fountain pen? Well, let me tell you, I just push this little button … whole room full of tear gas – ten seconds."

Billy, Sam's twelve-year-old happened to be in his dad's office. "Tell Mr. Fernandez what happened the other day."

"Now Billy, you just be quiet."

The entire story finally came out. Here's what happened: Sam was fooling with his 'pen' and accidentally pushed the button. As the room started filling with tear gas, Sam, the quick witted U. S. Marshal, whipped off the jacket of his suit, wrapped it around his new toy and threw it out the window.

Sam's office was directly above the Fairbanks Fire Station. When they saw what came out of Sam's window they quickly grabbed a very powerful water hose and blew Sam's jacket and gadget half a block down the street.

I don't know how Sam ever found the thing!

An Old Neighbor in Fairbanks, Alaska

Billy Barty, probably the best known of the little people since he appeared in numerous motion picture films as well as commercials (he was a midget), was born less than a mile away from my birthplace. I had never met him since he moved to California at an early age.

I was delighted to discover he was appearing at a night club in Fairbanks. I saw a few of his shows and to this day I can't understand why he never made it to the big rooms in Las Vegas. He was just flat out talented and funny.

Billy was kind enough to help our Baseball Program. He put on a little show where he played the part of a pitcher who didn't agree with the umpire calling balls and strikes. Billy chased the umpire around the bases, caught him at home plate and bit his knee.

Amazingly, Billy actually earned a letter in football at a small college in East Los Angeles.

On his last night in Fairbanks, he did the drinking chef routine. I knew he was actually drinking some serious liquor. He constructed a very large salad in a humongous bowl and ended by doing the backstroke in the salad bowl. More on Billy later.

Interesting Insights into Alaska Airlines

As the Fairbanks Sales Manager of Alaska Airlines I was able to learn, sometimes, more than I wanted to know about its inner workings.

For example: There were the pilots who partied, a lot. They were the guys who found it convenient when the airline was hauling a casket, whether or not it was occupied. Caskets would always be placed all the way forward in the main cabin. Movable curtains were used so passengers were spared a less than appealing sight.

The reason the partiers found it convenient: They'd place a couple of blankets over the casket and get some sleep in anticipation of the nights activities while the other pilot did the flying.

Since we were such a small company, informality was the rule. I was sitting in the co-pilot's seat one night on a Fairbanks-Seattle flight when we experienced a very exciting thirty seconds. Within that time span a buzzer went off indicating a fuel situation. The pilot had forgotten to switch tanks. Then the plane was struck by lightning. Fortunately, outside of some bouncing around, no damage.

Alaska used to fly contract flights within Alaska carrying aircraft fuel from Fairbanks to a remote location named Utopia. The airport at Utopia had one runway. Once a pilot had committed to landing, there was no option to change his mind and go around for another attempt since there was a large mountain at the end of the runway. While I was asked by the pilots if I wanted to go along for the ride to Utopia, I never accepted!

The Beginning of the End

Shortly after my first year in Fairbanks, Pan Am introduced new aircraft on the Fairbanks-Seattle route. They were pressurized and faster compared to Alaska's non-pressurized and slower craft. The competitive situation changed dramatically since the fare remained the same.

I asked the Alaska brass if we were going to match Pan Am. They said new aircraft were coming.

I waited for over a year. In good conscience, I couldn't ask my own brother to fly Alaska.

I resigned, reluctantly and went to work as a salesman for Airborne Freight Corporation based at San Francisco International Airport just south of the city of San Francisco.

Airborne

My First "Shaker"

After accepting a job that brought me to the Bay Area of Northern California, it took a while for me to relax. Having been born and raised in the coal fields of Western Pennsylvania, California seemed too good to be true.

In Millsboro, PA, the only time we saw any part of a palm tree was on Palm Sunday. Now they seemed to be everywhere. The weather was terrific, the Pacific Ocean nearby, beautiful mountains, The Golden Gate and Bay Bridges. I was overwhelmed AND apprehensive. Call it the Eastern Mentality if you want but I figured that anything this good HAD to have a downside.

Fortunately, my new job presented so many challenges I really didn't have time to let my mind wander.

My adjustment to a new environment was going pretty well until ... I was driving into San Francisco for a business appointment. As I approached the Fourth Street off-ramp it felt as if I was riding on tires that had suddenly gone flat. As I came to a stop at the bottom of the off-ramp, I saw a metal light pole moving back and forth.

It wasn't rocket science for me to understand I was experiencing my first earthquake.

I've never considered myself a brave person, but at that moment fear never entered my mind. My main thought? THIS is the kicker!

Mac

When I joined Airborne, the biggest shipper of air freight in the United States was the U. S. Air Force. One of the largest materiel centers originating this humongous volume was McClellan Air Force Base near Sacramento, CA.

The key to getting some of this business was the civilian traffic manager, a guy I'll refer to as Mac. He and I became friends through our mutual addiction to golf.

Mac's voice was just above a whisper. I never asked why. One day at lunch he told me the story, one of the most interesting I've ever heard.

Mac was in the Army during World War II, stationed in England. His throat was bothering him and a medical exam revealed a tumor.

He was transferred to Letterman Hospital in San Francisco. Further testing indicated surgery.

The Colonel who was going to operate told Mac he would perform a procedure that would tell him if the tumor was malignant. Mac would be conscious at the time and he would be told of the Colonel's conclusion. It would then be Mac's decision regarding removal. The Colonel had previously informed Mac that taking out the tumor meant that Mac would never talk again.

With Mac lying strapped to the operating table, the Colonel completed the initial procedure. After a short period of time, without telling or asking Mac ANYTHING, he went ahead and removed the tumor while either damaging Mac's vocal chords irreparably or removing them. Mac wasn't completely clear in that area.

The Colonel visited Mac regularly as he was recuperating. Mac would respond to the Colonel's questions by writing on a notepad. Mac said he ended every written answer with the words, "You son of a bitch."

After several days of lying there, depressed with the knowledge he would never speak again, Mac lost it.

The Colonel had told him that under no circumstances could he smoke or drink. So, Mac unhooked the tube or tubes he was attached to and found the nearest bar. Letterman Hospital was located on Van Ness Avenue, a main thoroughfare in San Francisco.

He drank a considerable amount of booze and smoked a cigar.

When Mac returned to his room, he couldn't sleep so he began reading a newspaper. Apparently, there are people who move their lips when they read. Mac was one of them.

As he proceeded to read he thought he heard the faintest sound. The next night Mac returned to the same bar, had a few more drinks and smoked another cigar.

73

Bottom line? We all have what can be referred to as dummy vocal chords behind our actual vocal chords. They serve no particular function. At that time Mac was one of a very small group of people who was able to produce sound from these dummy vocal chords. He subsequently went before groups of people who had lost their ability to speak and related his experience. I don't think he recommended the booze and the cigars.

When I knew Mac he could talk almost normally for fifteen or twenty minutes but then he couldn't talk at all ... so he chose to talk just above a whisper.

Due to a very real friendship between Mac and me, Airborne received a great deal of business from McClellan Air Force Base. I also called on other materiel centers in the southern and eastern U. S. with some success.

Turkey Eggs

While it wasn't generally known, the area around Sacramento, California was one of the largest producers of turkey eggs in the United States. Thousands upon thousands of pounds of those eggs were shipped by air to major American cities, particularly in the Midwest. The percentages of these eggs hatching successfully were very high.

As a sales representative for a San Francisco based air freight forwarding company, it was my job to get some of this business.

When I asked for the manager on my first sales call I was told he was out in the fields working. So, I tramped through the mud and who knows what else (it was spring) in my recently shined shoes until I saw a small group of men. When I reached their immediate area it was obvious how busy they were so I just nodded and watched the proceedings with considerable interest.

They were working in pairs. One man would hand a female turkey to another man who was holding what looked like a crude version of a hypodermic needle. He would turn the turkey upside down and swipe the needle across the turkey's genital area.

When they were through the manager approached me. I identified myself, touched lightly on my company's rates and service capabilities and suggested a follow up call when he wasn't so busy. He said, "Yes" and then we had a short chat.

I told him that never having seen the process before I found it interesting and could I ask him a simple question?

After he said, "Go," I said, "How do you get that stuff out of Tom?" He smiled, then said, "One of us just strokes him until it comes out."

I then asked, "And what does Tom think about that?"

He answered in a manner only a home spun, down to earth person could deliver. "Well, I'll tell you. It's the damndest thing to look down and see a turkey looking up at you with love in his eyes."

I chuckled all the way back to the office.

Bill and the Encyclopedia Salesman

Bill was the sharp, personable operations manager in Airborne's San Francisco office at the same time I was their general sales manager. In one of our discussions, he indicated his interest in sales and asked if I could give him information that would help him. I liked Bill and was happy to give him some of the basics I had learned. He then related an experience I found interesting and hilarious.

Upon answering his home's doorbell one evening Bill was greeted by a man selling Encyclopedia Britannicas. Bill was about to deliver a 'Thanks but no thanks' when he heard something familiar in the salesman's opening remarks. This prompted Bill to allow the man to enter and make his presentation. It didn't take long for Bill to realize this hopeful solicitor had read the same book on sales he (Bill) had read.

Feeling playful and perhaps a little sadistic, Bill decided to engage in a cat and mouse routine. The Britannica guy was the mouse. Every time the salesman tried to follow 'The Book,' Bill blocked his attempt. The salesman was becoming increasingly frustrated and puzzled at this potential customer's ability to seemingly anticipate everything he was going to say.

Bill knew this poor soul was reaching the end of the book's thesis. He also knew the last chance for success offered in the book was to choose an object in the room for which you would express the highest regard and admiration.

As Bill observed this man's eyes scanning the living room he was immediately aware he had chosen a sculpture of an African Warrior on the fireplace mantle, a gift

from Bill's mother-in-law and not one of his favorite furnishings. When the gentleman reached up to put his hand on the warrior Bill almost yelled, "Don't touch that!"

In a very short period of time, the books were gathered and a rather bewildered encyclopedia salesman was off into the night.

Number Three

I was promoted to General Sales Manager at Airborne. When the owner, John, and I discussed salary he told me he really didn't know how to handle the situation. He went on to say that in a short period of time my earnings had risen to a point near employees who had been there for many years. I found the process puzzling and disturbing and told him I just wanted to be treated fairly.

As time went by it became increasingly clear I didn't fit into John's management style.

I entered into discussions with the owner of another air freight company also based in San Francisco. I asked for the position of CEO plus equity based on the results I brought about. The owner agreed but I was still undecided upon leaving Airborne.

John and I were in a serious talk one day about my spending some time in New York in order to deal with some recently arisen problems. All of a sudden, out of context, he asked if I was considering leaving Airborne. I answered yes, but added I hadn't reached a final decision. He then asked for a loyalty statement. I told him I couldn't give him one and he fired me effective immediately.

I did make a deal with the other guy, but I learned that you lose a lot of negotiating power if you're unemployed. More specifically, our arrangement was verbal instead of on paper. After one year I felt I had held up my end of our agreement. I couldn't say the same about the other guy so I terminated the relationship.

The Mark IV's

Introduction

In analyzing the almost nine years of working with three companies I came to the conclusion I didn't do well in a corporate environment. Most of what I learned was from negatives. On too many occasions I was saying, "If this were my company, I'd handle it differently".

I considered going into education as a teacher (I received my B.S. in Education), but my brother, who had been teaching all of his adult life, cautioned that I might not do well in that environment either. He said it had very much the same problems as business.

So, I put all the money I had, $1200, on the line and started Mark IV Messenger Service. I had transferred to Los Angeles while on my last job so Mark IV Messenger Service, Inc., began in Hollywood, California, just up the block from the Hollywood Police Station.

Messengers Driving Lincolns

Mark IV would never have made it without a guy I'll refer to as Sandy. He held an important position with the largest messenger service in Los Angeles and left this position to join Mark IV.

We grew quickly enough for me to enter the big car stage, a white Lincoln with an aerial on the trunk so I could keep track of our truck movements.

I was at my desk one day when Sandy let me know that I had to play driver or Deluxe Lab, a large account, would have to wait twenty minutes on a rush shipment going to 20th Century Fox.

That was more than enough motivation to jump into my monster car, the worst vehicle I've ever owned, and GO. I pulled up to the main entrance of Deluxe, ran in, signed for the film and started to move toward my car. As I approached the door I saw Henry Goldfarb, the manager of Deluxe along with a visitor from New York (who can mistake that accent). As I passed them in the doorway, I heard the guy from New York say, "Goldfarb, I know this is Hollywood and you're all nuts, but messengers with Lincolns?" From Goldfarb, "What can I tell you?"

Billy Barty and the Little People

The friendship with Billy Barty that had originated in Fairbanks continued in Los Angeles. Billy was always "on." We were at lunch one day in the kind of restaurant that used big cloth napkins. Billy unfolded his, pulled it up near his chin and said, "Goodnight."

I learned a good deal about the Little People of America. As a group they have more physical problems than people of regular size. They also have more problems than average in becoming employed.

I decided to try and help with the employment part. Why not little people as messengers? After all, we were in Hollywood where the unusual is normal.

As a prototype, we chose one of Billy's friends, Herb Kinzel, who was actually smaller than Billy. We customized a blue blazer complete with a Mark IV crest just above the front pocket and topped his outfit with a snappy Tyrolean style hat.

After an appropriate training period we turned Herb loose. On his first day "soloing" I received a call from Dan Gannon, one of the bright young men who worked at NBC. From Dan, "I've heard about how you're trying to help Billy's friend but it's only fair I give you a play by play on an interesting experience."

"I was sitting at my desk when I heard a voice say "Mark IV." I looked towards the counter, didn't see

81

anyone and went back to work. Within a minute, another, "Mark IV." I figured someone was playing a game so I joined in by saying "O.K. come out, come out wherever (whoever?) you are". No response again then back to work just before another "Mark IV."

By now my curiosity was aroused. I walked to the counter, and looked down at the smiling face of this very small person.

From me, "Thanks for the call Dan."

A short time later, another call. This time it was Maurice Shapiro, a department head at NBC. Again, another "I understand what you're trying to do and I applaud your effort, but we had a little problem with your little person messenger. He was stuck in the freight elevator for a little while because he couldn't reach the down button. Just trying to help."

From me, "I appreciate the call."

In the final analysis, my project failed for a more simple, basic reason. These marvelous little people didn't have the stamina to get in and out of their car, and then walk to and from their pick up or delivery point several times in a relatively short period of time.

Pacific Air Freight

Mark IV's growth was accelerated by our forming a relationship with a small air freight forwarder, Pacific Air Freight, located in Seattle, Washington. We agreed to represent their company in the Los Angeles area.

Unfortunately, even though we were doing very well as Pacific's Los Angeles agent, Pacific was faring badly in their other offices.

In order to protect Mark IV's end of a very lucrative arrangement, I went to work for Pacific as Executive V.P. in exchange for fifty percent of their outstanding stock.

I knew that New York was the answer to Pacific's biggest problem, a quick, substantial increase in revenues. While serving as Airborne's general sales manager, I had hired a bright young man recently graduated from Stanford who was rather conveniently running Airborne's New York operation. We went for a walk on the upper east side of Manhattan and he agreed to join my effort. He and another friend of the past, a successful air freight trucker in the New York area, became the New York agents for Pacific. Their deal was exactly the same as Mark IV's in Los Angeles. New York's success was immediate and spectacular.

Once again I must use the word, unfortunately. Over simplified, the New York people and I had a profound difference regarding business ethics. Even though I was a major stockholder they prevailed with the top management of Pacific.

I was advised against a battle for control of Pacific so I sold my stock, terminated Mark IV's agreement with Pacific and started Mark IV Air Freight, Inc.

From a purely financial viewpoint my actions proved unwise. Pacific took over the original Airborne, became a distant third to UPS and Fed-Ex in the air freight business then sold out to DHL for a LOT of money.

The Second Mark IV

Mark IV Air Freight, Inc., was a moderately successful company for the nine years it was in existence. When we sold, our proudest achievement was never borrowing a nickel in a capital intensive business. All of our monies were generated internally and to say that starting and running Mark IV Air Freight, Inc. was an adventure would probably be an understatement.

In order to find a New York office, I walked every foot of the streets between the East River and Park Avenue from Twenty-Seventh to Forty-Fifth. We finally settled on a small place just off Third Avenue on Thirty-Fourth Street. This location had been a candy store. We didn't need much room since most of our freight consisted of small pieces from the entertainment and advertising industries.

We did have a few accounts in electronics. One of them was the Los Angeles area division of a company known in those days as Sperry Rand. I received a call one day from their traffic manager informing me that one of their shipments was late in arriving at its Long Island destination.

I called our New York office to find out the reason for the delay. The answer I received was bizarre and funny. The flight carrying this shipment was late arriving at JFK thereby causing our missing the Long Island delivery truck. The electronic instrument was worth some three hundred

85

thousand dollars and was too large to fit through the door of our office. But not to worry. Our innovative New York guy paid an alcohol impaired gentlemen three bucks to sleep on this expensive piece of freight on the

sidewalk outside our office. When I related these facts to my Sperry contact, I believe he literally fell off his chair laughing. The shipment was delivered one day late.

Government Workers (not the Brass) are Terrific

I've never understood why government workers have been subjected to so much criticism. My experience with these people, from the federal level down to the local, has been positive, without exception. When I say government workers I mean those who do all the work, NOT the brass.

Here's a specific example of why I feel this way.

When I decided to startup an air freight company, I knew the biggest initial hurdle was constructing a tariff. In addition to showing a company's rates and charges, it contains the rules and terms of carriage approved by the Federal Government along with describing the relationship between the air freight company and its customers.

Since our startup capital was minimal and constructing a tariff is quite expensive, the process became my responsibility. So, I went to Washington, D.C. and walked into the office of Tom Moore who supervised the cargo area of the Civil Aeronautics Board.

After introductory remarks Tom suggested, politely, that I reconsider becoming a principal in the air freight industry, that it was tough and very competitive. I answered that I appreciated his concern and welcomed his advice. I continued that I had evaluated the people I'd be competing against, knew some of them personally and felt I'd be alright. He shrugged and began asking about our tariff.

After a few minutes he excused himself and went into another room. When he came back he had some papers. As I sat there, he cut and pasted and shuffled his papers. In a matter of minutes he handed me a completed tariff. Had I contracted the work, the cost would have exceeded three thousand dollars.

Only a person with unique abilities could have accomplished this incredibly kind and generous gesture.

He wished me well and told me where I could find a low cost printer, recently arrived from Cuba who had set up shop in the basement of a red brick church within walking distance of his office.

I asked Tom if there was anything I could do to express my appreciation. He thanked me for the thought but indicated that the rules of his employment did not allow him to accept gratuities of any kind.

We kept a line of communication open and one day he said he was not far from retirement. I told him there was certainly a place for him in my company, but his Virginia roots were too deep.

After he did leave the government, I called and told him I still wanted to express my appreciation. What could I do? He finally said that he and his son had dreamed of attending a Washington Redskins football game but it was one of the toughest tickets in town.

By this time, Vince Lombardi had become the coach of the Washington Redskins. (Subsequent writings will explain how I came to know Mr. Lombardi.) I wrote and told him about Tom and his son. In a short time, I received two of Mr. Lombardi's personal allotment of tickets and then forwarded them to Tom. It took a while but I was finally able to say 'Thank you' for one of the most generous gestures I've ever received.

Since my experience with Tom Moore, every government worker from the copyright office, also in Washington, to the tax assessor's office, the passport people, and on, and on, and on, everyone was a positive.

I truly wish I could say the same about people providing goods and services in the private sector.

Doing Business in New York City

As the owner and CEO of Mark IV Air Freight it was my decision regarding our company's ethics. Even without moral issues, I knew that playing it straight was a sound, long-term business practice. No unexpected visits from tax authorities, no problems with the governing body of our industry and most important of all, a work force that knew they would be treated fairly.

On the downside we had to work harder than 90 percent of our competition since they didn't play it straight. Rather than go into detail on all the specifics I'll focus on just one, bribery. By bribery I mean cash, cars, vacations and women.

Since I've n ever understood what a CEO does in an office for ten hours a day I spent most of my time on the street in sales. This enabled me to understand that bribery was so common in New York City I mentioned it when I was meeting a potential customer for the first time. In polite language I asked the decision maker if he or she were 'on the take'. I also said there was no purpose in discussing Mark IV's rates and service if they were accepting goodies since that wasn't part of our package.

Somewhat surprisingly I never experienced any unpleasantness as the result of this question. I did experience moments that caused me to smile.

I once addressed the bribery situation to a young man named Raoul. He answered in the negative then quickly added he understood my question.

From Raoul: "Charley from Silver Wings said to me, 'Raoul, give me all your air freight business and we send you to Puerto Rico. Beautiful hotel, beautiful girls, everything FREE'." Raoul answered: "Sounds pretty good Charley. How about I go

down there, I think about it, I give you my answer when I get back?" "No Raoul, that's NOT the way it works. First your business, THEN Puerto Rico."

Max

Every time I visited a car wash not far from my office I noticed this small grey haired man that worked there. He stood out because he seemed to be working harder than his colleagues. Our trucking operation had grown to a point we had need for someone to load trucks at night for the next day delivery. This individual would also fuel and park the trucks. I asked Max if he would like to work for our company. He answered by asking, "How much would it pay?" When I asked him his wage with the car wash it was a very low number. I offered a substantial increase and he joined our effort.

It soon became apparent that Max was a much bigger project than I had anticipated. He never had a driver's license so we sent him to driving school. After completing this step he proceeded to fail his first two driver's tests. After he began working, I received word that a high number of dings and scratches began to appear on some of our trucks. I was then told that Max had been seen busily spray painting certain areas of our trucks. It was not a great beginning but things 'smoothed out' (pun intended) eventually.

When the process of selling my companies was nearing completion, I asked Max about his plans for the future. He didn't have any. During that time frame we owned a home in Pebble Beach, California. I asked Max if he would live in and take care of our

Pebble Beach place. For some reason, even though he was some years older than me, I felt responsible for him. He agreed. I then gave him one of our panel trucks and set him up with a job at one of Carmel's premier motels. I knew the manager, a very sharp lady named Kay.

Suzi and I were having dinner one night when I received a call from Kay. She said, "Frank, even though you have my complete trust I guess I need to be reassured. I introduced Max to our owners today and his reaction to the questions they asked him was catastrophic." I told Kay I wasn't surprised, that Max had a tendency to panic under pressure ... that in time, if she hung in there, he would grow on her and become a 'different' but valuable employee. That's exactly what happened.

We sold our Malibu home, moved to Pebble Beach, and Max lived with us for quite some time. Max never told you of an event or happening with any continuity. Here's an example: One evening he said, "I rolled the truck on my way to work, but I was only ten minutes late." Some five minutes later, "I guess I will have to pay for the tree."

On another occasion Max was hand watering the area in front of the Lobos Lodge. It was not unusual for his mind to wander. This was unfortunate for a nicely dressed lady walking down Ocean Avenue. What Max did to her couldn't be described as a sprinkling. It was at least a drenching.

When his place of employment was sold Max hooked up with a nice gentleman where he was given living quarters in return for taking care of the property.

We remained friends until his passing.

The Tonight Show

During the early years of my company, Mark IV Air Freight, the Tonight Show was broadcast from New York. Each year for a two-week period, Johnny Carson would broadcast from Burbank, California. Since there were no satellites back then, the actual tape of the Burbank shows had to be shipped to Manhattan where it was shown on a one-day delayed basis. This presented some interesting logistic challenges.

We had our best driver make test runs from Burbank to LAX but there was no way the elapsed time would allow us to pick up the completed tape in Burbank and make it to the airlines staging area before their cutoff time. I use the plural airlines since there were two tapes shipped each night as a precautionary measure and we had to use flights from two different airlines.

It didn't take rocket science to realize we had to use a helicopter from Burbank to LAX.

It took a LOT of planning and convincing for the wheels at NBC to accept our recommendation, which they resisted. By NBC wheels I don't mean the guys mentioned earlier in connection with the little people project. I believe these people were from New York and their main objection was cost.

Their reasoning was difficult to comprehend considering the total cost of moving the Tonight

Show from New York to Burbank for a two-week period. The cost of chartering a helicopter for ten days was petty cash stuff.

We finally got their approval where upon I told Sandy, my longtime associate, that this operation was so important that he should personally supervise everything from the studios in Burbank to the airlines staging area. Sandy gave me an immediate and firm NO. He would not get in a helicopter.

Even though I was a 'white knuckler' when it came to riding in aircraft, I couldn't in good conscience make an issue of his refusal.

So, on the evening of our first trip I was the one who arrived at the helicopter parking area a few minutes ahead of the pilot's arrival. There were two helicopters. One looked like a late model Cadillac, the other like an older model Ford. On the windshield of the 'Cadillac' was a note with the writing "Do not fly before calling..." I don't remember the phone number.

When the pilot arrived he grabbed the note, crumpled it and threw it away while saying something like, "They're always pullin' that stuff."

THAT scenario was not a confidence booster.

It was a short ride to the NBC Burbank parking lot. They were waiting for us. With the engine running I got out and ran, very low, picked up the tapes and hurried back to the helicopter.

As we left the San Fernando Valley the familiar night scene of greater Los Angeles lay before us and this guy is heading in a south easterly direction.

From me: "Hey, where are you going?"

The pilot: "To the airport."

"You're going the wrong way. See that brightly lit street down there? That's La Brea. That dark spot aways out is Baldwin Hills, and those blue lights way out there? That's LAX. Have you been there before?"

"No."

I'm thinking, GREAT. Now all we need is to fly into the landing pattern of a 747.

He made the necessary corrections and we landed at our first stop, the cargo area of United Airlines.

Sandy DID agree to meet me at United to be sure the tape was put on the flight.

When I gave Sandy the tape I forgot to ask him if he had any masking tape. I needed some to attach our paperwork to the shipment we were taking to the other airline. On the way out of United's cargo office I saw a brand new roll on a window ledge. I didn't have time to ask, I just grabbed it and ran. One of United's employees saw me take it and yelled, "Hey, bring back that tape." Then he saw me run to the helicopter in a takeoff mode. I speculated on what he was thinking: "Geez that was a pretty spectacular getaway just for the theft of a new roll of masking tape."

After nine more trips and after the Tonight Show went back to New York, the NBC people from Burbank asked me to come by. They presented me with a red scarf and a leather flyer's helmet, a la Charles Lindbergh.

The Teamsters

As Mark IV Air Freight continued to grow it was inevitable our truck drivers would become members of the Teamsters Union.

New York was forgettable, Chicago not so bad and Los Angeles was a kick because of a man named Raymond Frankowski. On our trip through life, everyone should be blessed with a friend like Raymond. He was smart, loyal, kind and funny.

Raymond's Entrance Exam

Raymond was a terrific football player out of East Chicago, Indiana who decided to play college ball for the University of Washington in Seattle. Here is Raymond's account of his admission process.

He was late arriving in Seattle. When he finally hooked up with the coach, a gentleman who would do WHATEVER it took to win, the coach informed Raymond that he had missed the test taken by most of the incoming freshmen. However, arrangements had been made for a special test to be administered by a professor known to be helpful to athletes.

After the usual introductions the professor said, "This is a simple one question test Raymond. How much is five and five?" Raymond couldn't resist playing and quickly answered "Twelve". The professor informed Raymond that unfortunately, he had failed whereupon the coach said, "Give him a break, he only missed by one."

The Polish Way of Pulling up Your Socks

Raymond, two other union officers and I were a foursome on the golf course from time to time. Friendly wagers were not unusual and gamesmanship was to be expected. On one occasion, I was almost into my back swing on the fourth tee at the club where I still belong. From Raymond: "Hey Fernandez, have you ever seen a Polish guy pull up his socks?" What could I do but stop and say, "No." I watched as this big man, with a face that any character actor in Hollywood would die for, unbuckle his belt, pull down his zipper and let his pants drop to the grass. The big cigar in his mouth just added to the picture. With his polka dot shorts flapping in the breeze, he then proceeded to carefully pull up each sock. It's not easy hitting a golf ball when you are laughing!

Speaking Before the Teamsters

Through Raymond I met and became friends with Andy who was way up there in the Teamsters hierarchy. Andy and I agreed on the direction the International Brotherhood of Teamsters should be taking, i.e., 'Straighten up and fly right'. There were forces building that could mean big trouble, even for an organization as strong as the Teamsters.

Andy arranged for me to go before a large gathering of his union's officials and deliver that point of view. It was amazing that I didn't hear one person booing, although it would be a stretch to say my speech received an enthusiastic response.

A Lesson Learned

While on the subject of labor matters, I once learned a valuable lesson from a negative experience.

Representatives of our messenger service once appeared before the National Labor Relations Board. They were defending the justification for terminating one of our drivers. We thought we would prevail but it wasn't even close. We lost. The next day I called a senior partner of the prominent labor relations law firm we had retained. I told him that we had been misled by his people regarding our chances of winning. I also suggested the attorney assigned to our case needed a lot more work. His response: He regarded me as a decent, honorable man. Therefore, he would accept all or any part of their final invoice of $5,000 as payment in full. We paid him $4,200, which is what I thought he deserved.

Some years later one of Mark Air Freight's customers claimed we had overcharged him by three thousand dollars. We had actually charged him exactly the rate on file, publicly, in our tariff. Over the years, we had become used to people, in emergency situations, saying, "Money is no object." They meant it until they received the bill. This particular customer was located in Reno, Nevada. I knew and liked the guy raising hell and I valued his business, so I decided on an in-person discussion. At the right time, I said to him, "I know you are a decent, honest man so I'll accept all or any part of that three thousand as payment in full." He looked at me, grinned and said, "You son of a bitch." I believe we settled for the full amount.

In Defense of the U.S. Postal Service

Like it or not, we live in a sound bite society. The influence of these sound bites on public opinion is difficult to calculate but I figure it to be strong.

For example: A talk show host recounts a news item about a special delivery letter being delivered some years after the addressee's death. I wonder how many people use that type of information as another reason to ridicule our nation's postal service.

In the interest of fair play, here's a story unknown to ninety-nine percent of every human being living in America when this story took place.

In pre-satellite days, a TV commercial in the form of a tape had to be in the TV station airing it. With its numerous, major ad agencies, New York City was the main origin for these commercials. Note: While most of these commercials went to TV stations, a small number went to other business locations. Our air freight company dealt with so many of the companies producing these commercials, I can assure you their product being completed on time was not one of their strong points.

When a phone call reached my office, it was usually important. I've never forgotten talking to the V.P. of one of America's largest ad agencies. This guy was almost hysterical. According to him, my

104

company had not delivered a very important shipment to their Detroit office. This commercial was the centerpiece of a presentation to a major auto manufacturer.

I checked with our operations department and they had not been notified to pick up this shipment. I called 'Old Yeller' and told him of my findings and suggested he

double check his information. He called in a few minutes, apologized and said the shipment was now ready for pickup.

An interesting but sad side note: We immediately dispatched a driver. While signing the paperwork, he was talking to the shipping clerk. For some reason our guy turned away for a few seconds. When he looked back to the shipping guy he wasn't there. As a result of the accumulated stress of the last couple of days, he had fainted and was lying on the floor half hidden by a table.

These commercials were shipped in padded 'Jiffy' bags. They were about six inches by eight inches and weighed less than a pound. It was a given they had to move by air.

Unfortunately, if you gave one of these Jiffy bags to an airline, the cost would be prohibitive due to a high minimum charge. Economics dictated the airlines preference for high weight shipments. Because of this preference the airlines had a tendency to mishandle if not lose small shipments.

With its expertise in handling a high volume of small shipments, the U.S. Postal Service was an attractive alternative. Economically, it was an air freight forwarders dream come true. The mailing charge for a Jiffy bag, Air Mail Special Delivery and a Returned Receipt was $1.38. The air freight forwarders charge to the customer ranged from $25-$50.

So, hundreds of thousands of Jiffy bags containing commercials left New York City by the U.S. Postal Service. It's important to note that these commercials were going to some remote towns like Harlingen, Texas and Thermoplis, Wyoming. They went to every town or city that had a TV station.

Now you tell me, if the U.S. Postal Service is so bad, how were all these shipments delivered in a timely manner with a minimal problem factor?

The time frame for all this activity was the 1960's when the Postal Services' processing and communications equipment was primitive compared to the present.

Finally, can anyone find a better bargain than sending a letter to any destination in the United States for forty-five cents?

Interesting Times in Europe

Dealing with Jet Lag

For one year, Mark IV Air Freight had a London, England office. On one of my trips there, I was accompanied by an employee and friend. He was the mad truck driver, Jim, mentioned elsewhere who now worked in Mark IV operations. Given the eight hour time difference between Los Angeles and London we decided before crashing to deal with jet lag by staying awake. When I discovered that Playboy had a club including a casino in London, I thought, great, that's where we'll spend our time.

In order to get into this establishment, we had to become members. Jim had the necessary ID on his person, I did not. It was a short distance to the hotel. I walked into the lobby around 3 a.m. Having lived in California for several years, I had developed a 'uniform' that I wore when traveling to cold climes and London's temperature certainly qualified for that designation. It was the middle of winter. This uniform consisted of a turtle neck sweater, what used to be called a car coat, complete with hood and wooden pegs instead of buttons. For a head covering I wore a navy P-cap given me by one of my sons. Wearing this uniform I walked into the elevator where I was joined by a Cary Grant kind of dapper gentleman who had imbibed a goodly number of drinks. As he gently swayed back and forth trying to light a cigarette, he took a good look at me and said, "I say old man, are you in from Switzerland?" (One of the best lines I have ever heard.)

Santa Claus and the Easter Bunny

Jim and I played a little blackjack then sat down for a drink. He had been drinking steadily, but you couldn't tell how much since the only telltale sign usually was a slight redness around the eyes.

For some reason, we started talking about our reactions to discovering there was no Santa Claus. I said it was no problem for me. We were so poor that a few nuts and maybe an orange in our stockings were about it and my brother and I knew our parents had put them there. With eyes turned misty by recalling his childhood, Jim said with considerable emotion, "Finding out about Santa Claus didn't bother me. It was the Easter Bunny thing that really beat the hell out of me." Getting up to hug him crossed my mind.

Fettuccini Alfredo

We had scheduled a two-day stay in Rome before heading home. After checking into the charming Hotel de la Ville near the top of the Spanish Steps, we decided to go for a walk. It was just about dark when we saw a restaurant sign saying Alfredo's. My first thought. Is this where Fettuccine Alfredo got its name?

There were two guys sitting on a bench not far from the entrance. One of them was dressed in regular clothing, the other in the uniform of a doorman. I asked them, "Is this a good restaurant?" The doorman looked at me, then said in Italian to his friend, "What kind of an idiot can this man be? He sees that I work for Alfredo's. What am I going to say? It's no good? Don't go there?"

The speaker didn't know I understood Italian. I couldn't help but chuckle when I said, "O.K., we'll give it a try, but it's closed. There are no lights." The guy in the uniform said, "Go, go," indicating we should go inside. What happened next I've never seen before or since. Within seconds of walking through the door, all the lights were on, the music system was activated and waiters were walking around with a towel over one arm. The restaurant looked as if had been open for hours.

The Fettuccine Alfredo was excellent. With the exception of cooking the fettuccine, the rest of the dish was prepared at our table. I never asked but it seemed our waiter was the proprietor of the place and a direct descendant of the original Alfredo. He was a genial little man with a waxed mustache that extended at least four inches on each side. He worked with large bright gold utensils and almost danced while doing so. While we were told this was the original Alfredo's, our sources were Italian. You take it from there.

Dino and the Carbinieri

The next time in Rome, I was traveling with another employee, Dino Digiorgio, our New York manager, a type-A personality if there ever was one. We had been at an 'if it's Tuesday, it must be Belgium pace' so a weekend in Rome was kickback time. The phone ringing beside my bed early on Sunday morning was not a positive contribution to rest and relaxation. When I picked it up, the caller identified himself as a front desk person and said, "Mr. Digiorgio, the carbinieri are here to see you." For those of you not familiar with 'carbinieri', it means police. I quickly replied, "This is Fernandez not Digiorgio, hold on." We had adjoining rooms so all I had to do was yell, "Hey Dino, pick up the phone." I could hear Dino saying, "What? What? That's impossible, impossible." Then some words I couldn't understand, then, "I'll be right down."

When he came into my room, he was beside himself. "I can't believe this. These people want to put me in the Italian army! I told them I left Italy as a young boy to go to America and that I served in the U. S. Military etc., etc. Their response was to say that for military service, once an Italian, ALWAYS an Italian." I lay there trying to hide a smile. I knew everything would turn out alright, so as Dino started to leave I couldn't resist saying, with a straight face, "Dino, I really regret adding to your stress factor but it's only fair I let you know this upfront. For purposes of seniority, my company does not recognize service in the Italian Army." First a look of disbelief, then, "How can you joke at a time like this? I'll see you."

We extended our stay in Rome while Dino made numerous trips between the American Embassy and the Italian authorities. Finally, the Italians said that they had

nothing more to say on the matter except that Dino should report to the military in Bari, Italy, his birthplace within a week.

We had been scheduled to go to Tel Aviv, then back to Milan before heading home, but I suggested that Dino leave immediately for Tel Aviv. I'd take care of Milan and see him in New York.

Unfortunately, Dino had a two-hour layover in Rome on his way back to New York and was understandably nervous every time he saw an Italian police person. I don't believe Dino ever returned to Italy!

The Ups and Downs of Flying

While the beginning of commercial jet travel was a terrific improvement over the slower, noisier prop jobs, for me, I've always wanted airplanes to be much faster.

I don't read or sleep when I'm in an airplane so my only out is an interesting conversation and 95 percent of the time that doesn't happen. However, there have been instances that could be called memorable.

The Little Boy on the Table

Upon entering the aircraft on one of the many flights I've taken, the first person I noticed was a little boy fast asleep on a table that was part of a lounge-like area. He appeared to be two or three years of age.

It seemed obvious that a woman sitting nearby was his mother. I stepped aside to let the boarding passengers behind me proceed, then said to the lady, "Of all the flights I've taken, all over the world, I've never seen a child his age asleep BEFORE the door was closed." The mother gave me a pleasant look that showed a twinge of accomplishment and said, "If I gave you the mickey I gave him, you'd be asleep too."

It's always nice to begin a flight with a smile.

Two Unusual Flight Attendants

There was a period in my life when I was at minimum, a top of the line hypochondriac. I had been working in Chicago when I experienced some unusual feelings in my chest. I immediately went to a medical facility for some x-rays. I then became so involved in my work I forgot to get the results until I was about to board an American Airlines flight back to San Francisco. I hurriedly wrote a note with the information necessary to contact a person in our Chicago office who would check the results of my tests.

To be sure the attendant could understand my note I began to read it. "Call Tom Kelly..." There were two flight attendants standing nearby and when I said 'Tom Kelly' they both yelled in unison "Tom Kelly!" I finished reading the note, thanked the attendant then turned to the attractive young ladies and asked, "Do you know Tom Kelly?" One of them said, "No, we just felt like yelling." We talked for a very short time and then the other one said, "When we get to cruising altitude, come up to first class and open the champagne for us."

I thanked them for the offer but I indicated I should keep my assigned seat in coach. This seat was located on the aisle.

A short time after the pilot turned the seat belt sign off indicating we had reached our assigned altitude, one of the ladies I had spoken to was standing next to me saying, "Sir, we do now have space available in first class, if you'll just follow me." I couldn't refuse since she had grasped one of my hands.

I must admit the trip seemed a lot shorter passing time with my new found friends.

About a month later I was on another American Airlines flight out of San Francisco. We weren't far from engine start up when I saw a familiar face — one of the ladies from the first class 'happening'.

When she saw me, in a voice that could be heard several rows away she said, "Oh no! Not you again." Passengers were rising out of their seats to see who she was addressing. Having originated many, many 'put-ons' I could easily recognize real quality and she had it. Just about the exact time when I was deciding on a response one of the engines on my side of the aircraft kicked in. An unusual amount of smoke came out and the pilot shut it down. My 'friend' had started to move down the aisle when I summoned her with a firm, "Miss." When she backed up I said, "I saw what happened with that engine and I want off this plane." She bought my show of concern and said, "But Sir, I'm sure it's nothing serious. We'll be on our way in a moment."

"Now look, will you please get my raincoat out of the overhead or do I have to make a real fuss?" I really couldn't deal with the truly worried look in her eyes. I had to smile whereupon she leaned close to me and quietly uttered some colorful words.

Unfortunately, I never saw either one of these marvelous people again. I use the word marvelous since I'm 100 percent for anyone who ventures 'outside the lines.'

Stevie Wonder

I was stretching my legs on a Los Angeles-Newark, N.J. flight one evening and paused for a moment at the back of the plane. It was a United DC-8 that had an area similar to a large booth in a restaurant. Seated at the table was Stevie Wonder.

I began a conversation with two people that I assumed were members of his group. You could describe our chat as just regular stuff. I remained there for a few minutes since I was in no hurry to get back to my seat.

One of the guys talked to Stevie for a short while then came back to me and said that Stevie would like to talk with me. I sat down beside him and engaged in an interesting conversation that lasted for almost two hours. It soon became obvious that Stevie was interested in asking me various questions as well as getting my opinions on different subjects.

At one point he asked me to put on a head set to listen to some material he had written so I could tell him what I thought of it.

I clearly remember one of his questions. He said he was performing somewhere with Bob Dylan and asked Dylan if he could borrow his harmonica. Dylan refused. Stevie then asked me, "Why do you think he did that?" I answered as honestly as I could by saying, "I don't have an answer. The next time you see Bob, ask him."

Close Encounters of the Best Kind

Elvis and the Ring

One of my sons, Jere, was one of the millions of people who adored Elvis Presley.

As Jere approached the 14th anniversary of his birthday, I decided to do something special.

On THE day I told him to pack a bag for an overnight stay. He didn't know why until we arrived at the Las Vegas Hilton where Elvis was appearing.

I have never been a heavy gambler and I didn't know anyone in Vegas so there was only one course of action. I determined that Emilio was THE guy — he had the power to let you into the showroom and to decide the location of your table.

I picked up what for me was a substantial number of chips. I don't remember their denomination but I believe they were fifties.

Emilio was sitting at his desk when I went into his office and introduced myself. I told him it was my son's birthday and wanted to make it a special night. He said he would be happy to do what he could. I thanked him and when I shook hands before leaving some of those chips passed from my hand to his. He gave me one of his cards (I still have it) with some letters in his handwriting.

About twenty minutes before show time, as we started walking to the entrance of the showroom, we couldn't believe the length of the line waiting to get in. It seemed to extend throughout the casino. We walked slowly; Jere was on crutches from an injury, to the showroom entrance. I showed Emilio's card to a gentleman who told us to go up some steps to the left of the head of the line.

Happiness for a young boy turning 14 was sitting front row center with a container of iced Coca Cola almost on the stage. As we left the showroom, Emilio was standing there. I thanked him for the marvelous seating. He bowed from the waist and said thank YOU Mr. Fernandez. When a guy in his position gives you that kind of action your first thought has to be "My God, how much did I give him?"

That night was the beginning of my becoming an Elvis fan. His charisma, his singing and the celebratory sound of the music were very appealing. From then on I was at the Las Vegas Hilton almost every time he appeared.

One of the staples of Elvis' shows was his passing out brightly colored scarves to his adoring fans. On this particular evening he changed his routine and began tossing stuffed animals to the people near the stage. There were hound dogs, teddy bears, etc.

One of them came in my direction. I reached out to grab it thinking it would be a terrific memento for Jere. I never touched it. A very athletic young lady literally executed an actual dive and claimed her prize.

I noticed a small object that landed on our table about the same time as the stuffed animal. I grabbed it and put it in the pocket of my jacket.

After things quieted down, I took it out. It was a ring. I'm thinking 'great,' probably costume jewelry and Jere will love it. Elvis usually wore at least three or four rings.

Just about then one of Elvis' people started walking through the audience yelling "Has anyone seen Mr. Presley's ring? That's a star sapphire and it's worth nineteen thousand dollars."

There was an 'interesting' looking guy sitting beside me. He said "You got it?" I nodded yes and he said "I won't tell." Anyway, when I heard $19,000, I stood and went over to Elvis, who was between songs. I handed him the ring and said "Elvis, here's your goody." He took it and thanked me.

The guy who was yelling said, "Thank God for an honest man." He came up to me, said the ring was a gift from the owner of one of the large casinos in Reno, Nevada and Elvis hadn't had it sized yet and that's why it flew off.

He also asked that I, and the people with me, come to Elvis' dressing room after the show. We had a couple of pictures taken and hoped we'd get Elvis' autograph.

When we arrived at Elvis' dressing room he was in the shower and we had a pleasant conversation with his father, Vernon. When Elvis came out he thanked me again, shook our hands and apologized for the sound of his voice that night. He said the cause was 'Vegas throat'. I assumed he meant the dryness of the desert air.

He came across as a decent, nice young man.

The most vivid memory of our meeting came when I asked if he would autograph our pictures. What I'm about to say is in no way an exaggeration. He lifted his arm above his head signifying that he wanted a pen. I would estimate his hand hadn't stopped moving and there was a pen in it. That's how closely his people watched him.

By the time we reached the showroom exit, the Hilton people working out front knew what had happened. The captain of the waiters referred to me as "The dummy that gave the ring back." That reference stuck for quite some time. I found it amusing.

Vince Lombardi

When Vince Lombardi resigned as coach of the Green Bay Packers and became their general manager, I felt that arrangement wouldn't last very long. He was too young (fifties), had boundless energy and a mind that wouldn't be challenged enough by a general manager's responsibilities.

As the CEO and majority stock holder of an air freight company, I felt that Mr. Lombardi would be the ideal candidate to replace me.

With the help of some exceptional colleagues, I had originated and developed this company to a point where it definitely had a future. Having met this challenge, I had begun to lose enthusiasm for my position. The way I looked at the situation, there were two main motivations to continue, power and money. Neither had any appeal. Added to the way I felt was anticipating what a kick it would be to work with a man like Lombardi.

So, our Chicago manager called Green Bay and was pleasantly surprised at the ease with which he set up a meeting for me.

It's not in my makeup to be nervous before meeting a person for the first time but I did feel the flapping of butterfly wings as I approached Lombardi's office. Respect is a very important word for me and I had enormous respect for him.

He greeted me at the door, took my raincoat and asked if it was alright to call me by my first name. I replied "Of course" but, I addressed him as Mr. Lombardi. I explained in detail the reason for my visit. While he was flattered by my offer, his first response was to indicate that he knew nothing about air freight. I explained that area could easily be taken care of within thirty days.

We spent the better part of an hour talking about our families and the Green Bay Packers.

It was difficult to differentiate between his gracious manner and real interest in what I had proposed.

I indicated my realization that he had probably been swamped with job offers. He confirmed this but indicated he would consider mine and would be agreeable to a second meeting.

When I did see him again, more pleasant conversation, then he said something that really is my reason for including this story in my writings.

He said he had come to realize that his heart was really in coaching. He continued that he was in the process of working out an arrangement that would allow him to do that.

Mr. Lombardi then said, "Most people don't know that the Packers are owned by the people of Green Bay. It's a nonprofit organization. When we have a good year, we put new rugs on the locker room floor or give something nice to the wives.

There are those who think I have a lot of money and I'm not complaining. I make a good living. But, any deal I make from now on will include equity."

Now, just think about this. Here was a man responsible for taking the Packers from at or near the bottom of professional football to the very top and keeping them there for a substantial amount of time. AND he did it with class and in a way that left a profound, positive impression on many of his players that endured through their lifetimes.

I can't put this forth as fact but I doubt that Mr. Lombardi thought much about his earnings throughout his tenure as the Packer's coach. One of the primary reasons for his

greatness was his ability to put EVERYTHING he had into his job. It seems to me his interest in money happened AFTER he accomplished his mission.

Fast forward to 2011 and think of the near absolute greed that permeates our entire society. One of the most prominent areas where it's so apparent is the area of sports. Allowing for rare exceptions, taking care of Numero Uno is the prevailing mentality.

In the ways that really count, on the positive side, I don't know of a situation in all of sports that can match the Green Bay Packer's story.

I consider myself to be so fortunate to have spent some time with the individual who was such an integral part of this story.

By the way, when Lombardi became coach of the Washington Redskins, a decent amount of equity was part of his contract.

Dr. B

While recalling my life's memorable experiences, I'd be looking over my shoulder if I didn't mention Dr. B.

For many years I was privileged to have a close friendship with him. Here's why I say I am privileged. If every person involved in providing medical services to the people of America possessed Dr. B's competence, his caring for others, his respect for and pride in his profession, and his value system, which placed the best interests of his patients first, we would not have a healthcare crisis in this country.

His motivation for becoming a doctor began as a young boy growing up in Russia. When a member of his family became ill, it was only natural a cloud of gloom would settle over the house. Then this man, their doctor, came through the door and the cloud disappeared.

This transformation left a permanent impression on Dr. B. If a doctor could have that kind of an effect on people then he wanted to become a doctor. When the family came to America, they settled in Omaha, Nebraska. Dr. B sold newspapers and in general worked very hard. He was befriended by a Catholic priest who later became a positive factor in Dr. B entering Creighton University. This was the beginning of the educational process culminating in his becoming an M.D. I was able to make that initial statement about Dr. B because he was that rare human being who traveled the precarious road to adulthood while acquiring very little "baggage".

In addition to his regular practice Dr. B worked with a company that insured motion pictures. His medical opinion on the health of a major star could shut down a production.

On the light side he once had a tough time convincing Marlon Brando he didn't have time to go down to street level and check out Marlon's motorcycle. Finally, while visiting Dr. B's office, Walter Mathau put on a white smock, positioned a stethoscope around his neck and took over. That I would have paid to see. Mathau was one of my all-time favorites.

Charlton Heston

Barbara B. was a very bright young lady who worked in a restaurant that I opened and closed one year later. We had some interesting philosophical discussions. For example, she once asked, "What's your take on religion? I've never heard you say anything about that area." I answered, "Having witnessed the beauty of Pebble Beach for all those years, looking at pictures of earth taken from outer space, and I know I'm stating the obvious, you wouldn't be human if the thought of a supreme power never crossed your mind. But more specifically I agree with the famous concert pianist, Arthur Rubinstein, 'If there would only be some sign'."

"What kind of sign?"

"There would be a light out over the Pacific Ocean from Mexico on the south to Canada on the north. This would be a light never seen before. It couldn't possibly have come from anything manmade. In the center of the light this face would appear."

From Barbara, "Charlton Heston, right?"

John Wayne

In the time frame when I used to visit Las Vegas frequently, I would, on occasion, set personal records for staying awake. Somewhere around 2:30 - 3:00 one morning I was hanging out in the casino of the El Cortez Hotel on Fremont Street when I saw John Wayne and another gentleman approach one of the crap tables. At that time of the morning there weren't many people around so it was easy to stand nearby. A marvelous opportunity to do some 'people watching'.

John covered the numbers and the only other player at the table began throwing the dice. He kept them for a considerable length of time, which meant that John had won an appreciable amount of money. After the shooter threw a seven, the stick man moved the dice in front of John. John said, "Hell, give 'em back to the Chinaman."

The 'Chinaman' then flashed a brilliant smile and said pleasantly, "I'm Hawaiian, John." John said, "Whatever."

Stealing a Horse in Downtown Chicago

Having completed a productive week in the Chicago area, our newest sales trainee and I decided to celebrate by having dinner at a well-known mid-city restaurant. Afterward we were strolling down State Street, that great street, when a young man at the reins of a for-hire carriage slowed near us. He asked if we would care to go for a ride. It was a nice September evening and we were enjoying our walk so I declined, politely. With an easy manner the driver persisted. I again declined. Then he said "C'mon it's free." The free part didn't motivate me but I was curious as to WHY he would make such an offer. Over the years it's been my tendency to satisfy my curiosity. So, we climbed into the carriage.

Here is his story and I believed every word: He was from a small town in Arizona on his way to South Bend, Indiana to register for the fall term at Notre Dame. He had a lengthy wait for the train and spent some of his time walking on Michigan Ave. Having grown up around horses he stopped when he saw the horse and carriage parked in front of a hotel and began a conversation with the driver who apparently had something going with a young lady in the hotel. So, the young Arizonan, after promising he wouldn't be gone for very long, was permitted to give the horse a little exercise.

The combination of a large city plus a little liquor and we're talking LOST.

Because I believed him, combined with my being a fan of the Notre Dame football team since I was nine years old, plus his being so straight-forward and just plain nice were sufficient reasons for me to ride (so to speak) to the rescue. I told the young man to continue on State Street until I saw a place that might have a telephone.

In the meantime, I looked around the carriage until I located the name of the carriage company, Ye Old Carriage Company.

A small delicatessen was our first try for a phone and it was successful. My friend stayed in the carriage. I looked up the number and even though it was a Sunday, a gentleman quickly answered. I related our situation. He said "No problem." Turns out the barn was a few blocks away on North Wells Street.

I went out to announce our good fortune. My friend, Richard, was standing on the sidewalk alone. When I asked, "What happened?" I was told that a drunk and his lady friend had come along and wanted to go for a ride and the kid obliged.

At that point it would have been easy to say, "To hell with it." However, in addition to being a curious fellow, I also don't give up easily.

After confirming the direction 'they' had taken I told Richard my plan. "Let's think positive and assume he took them for a ride around the block. So, we'll go the opposite direction and hopefully meet up."

When we turned the corner we saw the horse and carriage, our new found friend, the drunk and his lady, two police cars and a crowd that was growing, rapidly.

I went up to one of the cops and told him exactly what you've read.

He gave me a questioning look and said, "You mean to tell me you're going to all this trouble to help someone you met thirty minutes ago?" I simply said, "Yes" and from the look on his face I really didn't think he was buying my story. I was trying to think of another approach when another police car pulled up and out stepped the original operator.

As soon as our new found friend identified him I approached the policeman I had been talking to and said, "Would you please ask that man — pointing to the original driver — if he gave his permission for this young man to go for a ride?"

The policeman hesitated and then acted upon my plea. It was a pleasant surprise to hear this guy say "Yes." With that, all of the policemen conferred for one minute then rather hurriedly placed HIM in one of the police cars.

I shook hands with the young man from Arizona and wished him success at Notre Dame, the drunk and his lady friend stumbled into the night and Richard and I continued our walk.

Empathy for Richard Nixon?

I had another interesting experience on a commercial airline flight. On my way to Chicago from Los Angeles I spent a day with family members in Phoenix, Arizona. Being seated in the middle of a three seat arrangement wasn't my first choice on the Phoenix-Chicago segment but things began looking up after introductory remarks indicated the guy in the window seat was Nick Timmisch, the Washington D.C. Bureau Chief for Newsday. Nick had been interviewing presidential candidates and was in Phoenix for a meeting with Barry Goldwater. While I had some interest in his impression of Goldwater as well as other candidates, I finally said, "O.K. Nick, here's the big one. Tell me about Richard Nixon." Nick responded, "Rather that verbalizing my thoughts I'll let you read an article I wrote."

I remember clearly the difficulty he experienced going into his briefcase. He wore a cast on one of his hands.

It was the best article I've ever read about Richard Nixon. Rather than reflect on the time-worn aspects of Nixon's background, Nick's main point said that Nixon was practically struck dumb in the presence of John Kennedy. Why? Kennedy was wealthy. Nixon was not. Kennedy's appearance was striking while Nixon's was ordinary. Kennedy was a charmer. Nixon was not. Kennedy exerted a high degree of confidence. Nixon did not.

Once empathy replaced disdain it was easy for me to recognize Nixon's pluses. Perhaps the most prominent — his understanding of the importance of thinking globally.

Opening the door to China was a well-remembered indicator of this thinking. Unfortunately, flaws in Nixon's makeup resulted in his resigning as President. Subsequent revelations about Kennedy were hardly flattering.

Notre Dame

I've been a fan of Notre Dame football since I was nine years old. Living in Fairbanks, Alaska, pre satellite, I had one wall of my apartment lined with radio equipment trying to bring in Armed Forces Radio Service. They broadcast some of the Notre Dame games. Then a bell rang. Since I was so involved in civic affairs, I got to know Bill Snedden, the publisher of the Fairbanks Daily News Miner. I asked Bill if I could represent his newspaper and report on a Notre Dame game. I would actually write a story that would appear in the sports section. He quickly said, "Of course," and I was off and running. Since I worked for an airline, transportation was no problem. Alaska Airlines to Seattle, Northwest Airlines to Chicago, and the South Shore Rail Line to South Bend, Indiana.

I walked up to the press window. When the young man asked, "May I help you?" I said, "Frank Fernandez, Fairbanks Daily News Miner." The young man said "What?" Once again I said, "Frank Fernandez, Fairbanks Daily News Miner and I'm here to cover the game."

"Did you wire ahead for space in the press box?"

"No, I didn't realize you were supposed to do that."

"This is one of the biggest games of the year and since you didn't let us know ahead of time you were coming, I'm afraid we can't help you."

"I've come an awful long way. Isn't there anything that can be done?"

"There is only one person in the world that can help you."

Hopefully, "Who is that?"

"Charley Callahan. Unfortunately, he's up there."

He pointed to the press box then said, "See those two big guys standing over there on each side of the elevator? They're freshman football players and their job is to let NO ONE into that elevator without proper credentials."

After thanking him for his time I walked over and began talking to the guards. Once again, I explained the long distance I had traveled and my affections for Notre Dame. They were kind enough to let me into the elevator. When I stepped into the press box, I asked the first person I saw, "Can you point out Charley Callahan?" He pointed and said, "The guy with the brown fedora on the back of his head." Charley was obviously a very busy man but I got his attention. I introduced myself and asked if I could have a seat in the press box. His first reaction was amazement at what he was hearing, then, "Never mind 'Can you have a seat' how in the hell did you get up here?" I quickly offered that the two young men felt sorry for me and that I would greatly appreciate his going easy on them. He then pointed to an empty seat and suggested I get the hell over there. I ended up sitting a couple of seats away from Arch Ward, the famous sportswriter of the Chicago Tribune.

My report did appear in the Fairbanks Daily News Miner and I remember thinking how neat it would be to have a job covering college football games. Free hot dogs and a good part of the story you wrote was given to you at the end of each quarter in the form of a sheet of paper that contained all the action of that quarter. I also covered the Notre Dame-Iowa game in Iowa City, Iowa. This time I did wire ahead for space and everything went without incident.

Cary Grant and the Magic Castle

Suzi and I were members of the Magic Castle for a few years. I guess you'd call it a marvelous club where magicians hung out as well as entertained in a number of small show rooms. It's located in a picturesque building on the hill above Franklin Avenue near Orange Street in Hollywood, California.

They present a marvelous buffet and you can press a button that moves a wall allowing you access to the main area. They also have Irma the Magic Piano. Anyone can play a few notes on Irma and magically it will play the rest of the song you began. The idea is to stump Irma. I approached the challenge with enthusiasm and played a few bars of a rather obscure tune called 'Robin's Nest'. Irma couldn't pick it up. As we were cheering our success, Irma played her version of 'Nobody Likes a Smart A--.'

One evening we were enjoying a show being put on by a magician who was also very funny. It was a small room with seats that went up several feet instead of out. We were sitting down in front. Suzi is a pretty woman so it wasn't surprising for the performer to ask her to assist him in this particular feat of magic. Little did he know what was going to happen. As he completed this particular trick, Suzi, who wanted to know how he did it, grabbed his arm and said, "How'd you DO that?" The magician good naturedly said, "Please, would you grab Heifetz' arm while he was playing the violin?"

As we were leaving, none other than Cary Grant was coming down the steps from one of the upper rows. As he neared us, he flashed that brilliant smile and said, "H e l l o, Suzi." A surprising end to an enjoyable evening.

My Neighbor Leo

Through information from my children, I knew the guy next door worked in the entertainment business. Primarily because of our vocational efforts we weren't around much and had never met until the day we had this interesting conversation in front of Leo's house. Even though I'm known for talking, I'd much rather listen if what I am hearing is interesting and this guy was interesting. I discovered later he was a well-known director, with a very well-known TV series among his credits. Leo was completely without pretense, just a nice person who came across as absolutely believable.

He asked if I had read the book, The Godfather. I replied in the negative and he suggested I get a copy.

In answer to one of my remarks, he confirmed how upset Frank Sinatra was because of Mario Puzo (the author of The Godfather) creating a character with more than a little similarity to him (Sinatra). Leo also related that the word around town said that Frank wanted to be a 'Don'. For those not familiar with the word, Don, it more or less applies to an important person in the Mafia. He then spoke of an instance where Sinatra's actions looked very much like a Don's.

It happened after the Frank Sinatra-Ava Gardner divorce. As often as not, when Ms. Gardner chose to end a relationship she would leave the country. Spain was usually her destination.

One of her rejected suitors was not the type who gave up without a struggle so he traveled to Barcelona, Spain to see Ms. Gardner. As he was walking through the lobby of

the hotel where she was staying, one of the two men who were in the lobby approached this gentleman and explained it would not be beneficial for his health if he entered the nearby elevator. Notwithstanding the divorce, those men worked for Sinatra. Frank, like members of the Mafia continued to look out for those they are, or have been close to. It was public knowledge this particular guy was a heavy drinker with a violent temper. Leo never mentioned him by name, but I could have made a good guess.

Being in such close proximity, my children knew and played with Leo's children. One of them (Leo's, not mine) is currently a major movie star.

The Lady at the Tuck Box

When we lived in Pebble Beach, the Tuck Box was a well-known tea room in downtown Carmel. Being fond of their scones and omelets, I was in there often enough to have a good relationship with the manager. It was a small place with a busy luncheon trade, so it was not unusual to accommodate their customers by seating them at a table already occupied. I was usually alone so I met some interesting people.

Of particular note was this charming older lady. At one point our conversation centered on her efforts to affect a wise investment strategy. Upon her request a young financial counselor visited her home. This individual knew my luncheon companion was a person of considerable means and he was being careful and formal in trying to obtain her business. At a certain point in their conversation she related how the young man said to her, "May I please inquire to your main motivation for the investments you are contemplating?" She quickly and straightforwardly replied, "Greed sonny, greed."

It's interesting how the truth has a tendency to raise hell with formal, stuffy presentations.

Observations of a People Watcher

Ladies of the evening = 4 - The guys = 0

Gentleman B

One of my colleagues and I once traveled to Tokyo on business. At the end of our first workday, he suggested we go out on the town and find some 'action'.

As a strong believer in logic and reason I then asked B., "May I describe 'action' to the ultimate? He gave a somewhat hesitant, "O.K."

"We would go to a bar or club and meet a couple of attractive, desirable women who were not 'professionals'. We would then pair off and go the 'your place or mine routine.' A memorable sexual adventure would result. Is that an accurate description?"

From B. once again hesitantly, "I guess so."

"May I ask one more question?" I said.

After another nod, "In all the years of looking for 'action' has anything remotely close to my description happened?"

"No," said B.

"Please pardon my scientific approach ... just trying to save you some time and money."

I wished him well and he left.

While B. was a seeker of action, he was, to put it mildly, a frugal person.

After my companies were sold, B. became a consultant and developed some business in Tokyo. While having dinner he told me an easily remembered story.

A reliable source in Tokyo informed B. that "for hire" ladies in Taiwan were financial bargains. This was enough of an incentive for B. to schedule a layover (pardon me) in Taiwan instead of taking a Tokyo-Los Angeles non-stop.

In addition to being frugal, B. was a cautious fellow. Before 'bedtime' he felt it wise to take a few penicillin tablets. Also, when the young lady offered to hang his clothing he declined. Trying to be civil, he indicated that he had developed the habit of arranging his clothing at the bottom of the bed.

Amazingly, I didn't comment on his remarks. After the inconvenience of stopping in Taiwan, he bedded his bargain while worrying about being robbed and experiencing considerable dizziness (part of B,'s story) caused by ingesting the antibiotics.

Gentleman A

The fact there were two 'working women' in Fairbanks was common knowledge. My friend A. decided to retain one of them. This decision included treating the occasion as a regular date.

So, he took his date to a restaurant a few miles out of town for drinks and dinner. When you're a few miles out of Fairbanks in the dead of winter nothing good is likely to happen.

A. hadn't calculated the numbers properly — after paying the restaurant bill he determined the cost for the lady's services. He couldn't come close. A. then asked if she would take a check. The answer was a quick and resounding "No!" He then asked if she

would lend him cab fare back to town. I believe her answer was on the order of "Get lost you creep."

Guess who received a phone call? I really considered saying no but what are friends for?

It's fair to assume that A. would never forget that evening, however...

On another occasion, we had just come out of a Frank Sinatra performance at the Sands in Las Vegas and decided to have a night cap. A short time after settling in at the bar, two became four with the arrival of two women. The one that sat beside me was attractive. After acknowledging her presence, I explained I didn't want to insult her in any way, but

I really was old, tired and very married ... in other words, a waste of her time. She found my honesty refreshing and decided on an extensive conversation.

After a while, I excused myself, I really was sleepy. I told A. I was going to my room. We agreed to meet for breakfast.

The next morning I asked if he had decided to buy. He said yes, that it had been pleasant, that she had given him a massage until he fell asleep. She departed with his money. As an afterthought, he added that she had left him enough cash for breakfast.

Gentleman E

Then there was this individual who we'll refer to as E., who worked for Alaska Airlines in Anchorage, Alaska. It was a short flight from Fairbanks and I would jump on any decent reason to take that trip. My main motivation? A Chinese restaurant that featured a fantastic New York steak.

After yet another enjoyable evening at this delightful eatery, E. suggested we visit a place called the Polar Bar — an apt name for an Alaskan establishment.

When we entered, there was one woman sitting at the bar drinking a can of beer. E. walked up to a point directly behind her, put his arms around her waist and began whispering into her ear. As subsequent events indicated, E. didn't know her. The lady showed absolutely zero reaction to E.'s romantic overture for a couple of minutes. Her first movement was to crush the beer can with what appeared to be minimal exertion. In that time frame beer cans were made of much heavier metal than the present cans. As a serious people watcher, I was fascinated.

I told E. I was going back to my hotel and left.

Some considerable time later, I was awakened by a call from E. Like A. he was unable or unwilling to meet the price and was very concerned about his well-being. From what I remembered, this woman could inflict some serious damage to E.'s body with one hand (E. was a short, slight person). E. asked that I call him back to inform him his mother was gravely ill thereby giving him a reason for a quick exit.

    I didn't make the call. When I saw E. the next day there were no visible signs of injury.

GOLF STORIES

Jack Nicklaus

In 1970, I decided to introduce a new concept in transportation consulting to a select number of potential clients. Eighteen holes of golf on a premier course seemed a good way to achieve my objective. The idea would be to maximize the chances of getting key people from the list I had prepared to attend this event. By key people, I mean chief financial officers and up representing companies with annual sales from fifty million to one billion dollars.

I imagined myself as one of these key people and asked, "What would be my reaction to receiving an invitation from someone I'd never heard of to play a round of golf? Even if the invitation included roundtrip transportation to Scotland, Hawaii or the Bahamas, would I be interested?" My conclusion was, no, I would not. Number One: As the CEO of a multi-million dollar company, I'm a sought after individual on a regular basis. Number Two: My personal financial status would allow considerable latitude in where I chose to play. There had to be a kicker.

In those days, a young lawyer in Cleveland, Ohio named McCormack had begun a sports management firm and represented Jack Nicklaus, Arnold Palmer and Gary Player. My research indicated I could hire one of these individuals to co-host this golf day.

I called Mr. McCormack's firm and spoke to one of his colleagues, Chuck Foley. I asked if Mr. Palmer was available for a contemplated date in the third week of October. Mr. Foley said he wasn't but what would I think of retaining the services of Jack Nicklaus. With no hesitation or disappointment, I said okay.

For those who know what a famous golfer commands these days for appearing at such a function, imagine retaining him for $7,500 with $3,500 up front and the remainder after the event.

The invitations then went out on Golden Bear stationery asking if my targets would join Jack and me for eighteen holes.

Since I was based in Los Angeles in those days, there were some pretty fair courses to consider as possible sites, but I zeroed in on Riviera Country Club when I was told they would, on occasion, provide their facilities for such an event.

I don't remember the name of the gentleman I called at Riviera, but I do recall a rather chilly response. Something on the order of, "Well, you know, this is a highly respected old-line establishment..."

At that point, I told him I understood how careful one had to be, particularly in Southern California. I further stated that rather than check me out, would it help if my co-host was Mr. Nicklaus?

First silence, then I thought I heard a gulp. Then I did hear, "Jack? Nicklaus?"

I allowed he was the only Nicklaus I knew. Then, rather quickly, "Well, under certain circumstances..."

We arranged a meeting and finalized the details.

I had been informed by Mr. Foley that Monday was the preferred day and everything was set. The response from the invitations was positive and we were in a "Go" position until I received a call from Cleveland on Saturday, two days from THE day.

Chuck advised me that we had a potential problem. He had just spoken with Jack who was playing in a tournament in Northern California. Because of a day's rainout,

there was a possibility that Jack would be playing on Monday. Foley suggested I call Jack and get a status report. Up to that point, I had never spoken to him. I called and was greeted warmly by that distinctive voice. When I asked what was happening, he said he'd pushed the button prematurely. The tournament people had scheduled 36 holes on Sunday but there wouldn't have been a problem anyway since he'd missed the cut. Jack also indicated he was really looking forward to playing Riviera since it would be his first time there.

I clearly remember meeting his chartered Lear Jet on Monday morning at LAX Executive Terminal. In anticipating Jack's arrival, I had been mulling over what I would say to him while conversing. I've never been much for small talk. I had done a little reading about him and was able to ask if it was true that he had fainted at the birth of two of his children. He nodded in the affirmative and then offered that he had spent about as much time in the recovery room as Barbara.

Looking back on that ride to Riviera, I realize now that what I said next could be considered presumptuous if not in bad taste. My explanation would be previously indicated abhorrence of small talk along with a tendency to shoot from the lip.

I explained to Jack that one of my idiosyncrasies was a game I played where I would develop theories about people I'd never met and then hope I could establish their accuracy. When these theories concerned people in the public eye, validation could only result from reliable information provided by the media or from meeting someone who knew the subject of my theorizing. In this case, I was in a position to prove or disprove this particular theory from the person with the best qualifications!

I then asked if he would mind answering a couple of questions. He said no, that it was all right. Then, "I get the impression you're about ready to say goodbye to McCormack."

With that, Jack straightened up a little, looked me in the eye, hesitated for a moment, then said, "Yes, that's right."

To the best of my knowledge, up to that moment, I had not seen or heard of any information that gave any indication of what Jack had just verified.

I followed with, "Okay, one down and one to go. May I give you my theory of why?"

He told me to go ahead and I said, "Because you believe you can do anything he's doing for you as well as he can, maybe better."

Once again he indicated I was right. I mentioned this not to impress anyone with my theorizing powers, but to indicate the candor and openness of this man with someone he had just met.

After arriving at the course and sampling the sumptuous continental breakfast provided by the Riviera people, we went down to the driving range where Jack conducted a clinic for some 45 minutes.

Once I was "in" for several thousand dollars, I decided I might as well invite a few of my friends.

Jack was hitting 8 iron shots when one of these friends asked him when he started his down swing. Jack gave him a look that conveyed humor and feigned disgust, then answered, "Usually, when I finish my back swing."

As simple as that may sound, I can't tell you how many fellow slashers I've helped by telling them they should have a sense of completing their back swing before starting down — so many of us bring the club down before our movements even begin to look like a swing.

160

After the clinic, we walked up to the first tee to begin play. I had decided to join Jack on number ten, hoping that playing nine holes would lessen my chances of playing pathetically with Jack looking on.

Jack's appearance at Riviera had not been publicized. When word circulated that he was on the premises and about to begin play, everything stopped and practically everyone started moving toward the first tee. One of the few who went about his business was Dean Martin. He paused briefly to say hello to Jack, acknowledged Jack's introduction of me, then continued toward his practice area.

By the time Jack was ready to go on the par-five first hole, a small gallery was watching. Several asked that he try to drive over the barranca, a 300+ yard carry. He was happy to oblige and succeeded on his second try.

The last time I had spoken to Cleveland, Chuck suggested that I not ask Jack to move around much on the course, that is, have him play with just a couple of threesomes. On the way up the hill to the first tee, Jack asked if I wanted him to drop back on every hole so he could lay with everyone in attendance.

When I did join Jack on number ten, I wasn't any more prepared than I would have been on number one. I mean, what's a hacker to do when HE is watching. I put my drive into a fairway bunker on the left. HE stood above me and said, "Just get it out, Frank." Happily I was able to comply.

161

On my way to the green, I started to analyze my self-loathing regarding my ability to play golf, particularly when compared to HIM.

I am happy to report my brain was functioning well enough to come to the following conclusion: Jack couldn't sell transportation as well as I could. That was my chief vocational effort. (At the time I was the owner of an air freight company and a trucking company.) Jack's chief vocational effort was playing golf.

Whether it was the height of rationalization or what, it worked. On number eleven, a par five, I hit a decent drive, a good fairway wood, put my wedge about twelve feet and sank the putt. Jack asked if I made birdie and in my newfound confidence, I answered, "Is a birdie one less than par?" From there on I played reasonably well.

After finishing his round, Jack waited in an area not far from the 18th green and had his picture taken with every individual in attendance. It was interesting to note that every picture of Jack was a good one.

For those of you that might be considering such an event: I had each photograph pressed into a piece of mahogany, placed a gold colored plate with pertinent information regarding the event inscribed underneath, then presented the plaque to the individuals I later called on.

At the dinner culminating this golf day, I made a short speech to my prospective clients. I told them I

162

had a concept that was certain to benefit their companies. I further stated that I wasn't going to commercialize what had been a memorable day except to say, "If you received a positive impression from those of us who put on this day, please say yes when my secretary calls for an appointment. As for myself, I just had a great time

and thank you for coming." At least that's what I think I said. I was on such a high, fueled by happiness because the day had gone so well, i.e.:

- ☐ Jack was a fantastic co-host
- ☐ The weather, even by Southern California standards had been spectacular.
- ☐ The golf course and the services provided by Riviera were top of the line.

After my short speech, Jack was kind enough to stand and say that as we might imagine, he had attended quite a few functions of this nature and he couldn't remember one he enjoyed more.

Later, when all the guests had gone, a couple of my colleagues, Jack and I had a nightcap and talked about numerous subjects.

Oh, by the way, all of my expenses were covered and then some by the revenues received from just one of the companies whose representative was in attendance.

Finally, a little reflecting on this man named Nicklaus. Some years ago, a fellow wrote a book called, In Search of Excellence. When it comes to Jack Nicklaus, the term is, Excellence Found.

As a result of that day at Riviera plus what I've learned from watching, reading and hearing about him, this is one impressive human being. I believe I'm qualified to make this statement since I've looked for real excellence all of my adult life: Excellence in the vocational sense (very hard to find) and excellence in the overall makeup of individuals. One of the reasons I've rarely found it is the fact that I am at the opposite end from those who participate in the "perception is reality" phenomenon so prevalent in our society. I've always tried my best to employ objectivity and honesty in this search for excellence. With this background, I don't hesitate to make the following statement:

In the history of professional sports, I don't know of anyone who has matched Jack's record of overall excellence.

In the same time frame, HE:

- ☐ As husband to Barbara and father to his children has done his best to contribute positively to the all-important family values we hear so much about these days. I remember a specific instance when minutes after finishing his final round, he traveled by helicopter from Pebble Beach to San Francisco Airport for a flight to Japan so he could maintain a self-imposed time limit away from home.

- ☐ Became the best player, quite probably, that the game of golf has ever known.
- ☐ Developed a business empire of considerable magnitude.

Hell, in all my years of people watching, I don't need one hand to count those who have pulled off just two: family and business.

When you consider the concentration and focus necessary to play golf at Jack's level, his overall success goes into another new dimension. AND, he has done all of this with grace and class. The words, "grace and class" have particular significance when you think of the way he took the heat he received from "Arnie's Army" when he was taking over as Numero Uno.

Of one thing I am certain: Don't figure on seeing another like him any time soon.

The Marvelous Kiwis

In his early twenties, Bob R. once won five amateur tournaments in a row. Two of them were the California State Amateur and the National Publinx. We signed a contract thereby formally pooling our efforts to get Bob on the PGA tour.

In order to gain valuable experience, Bob embarked on what was literally an around the world tour. In those days good American players had no problem entering important tournaments in foreign countries.

Based on a spur of the moment decision I decided to watch Bob play at Paraparam Golf Course in Wellington, New Zealand.

As I drove into the golf course parking lot, two gentlemen dressed in their Sunday best were coming out of the clubhouse. When I pulled into a parking space, one of them informed me my left front tire was nearly flat. I thanked him and hurried into the clubhouse to get Bob's starting time so I could determine what hole he would be playing. When I came out to change into my golf shoes, these two gentlemen had taken off their jackets and were busy fixing my flat! (I had left my keys in the ignition.)

In New York they would have been fighting over the parts.

This act of unusual generosity set the tone for the time I spent in this marvelous country. I can't say enough good things about New Zealanders.

Whoever Breaks a Window

Open space was very limited in Millsboro. Quite often our softball games were played on a street running through a residential part of town. All of the houses in this area were close to the street so broken windows were not unheard of. For no particular reason, we developed a rule that applied when a batted ball was headed for a window. If someone yelled, "Whoever breaks it pays for it," everyone but the batter was home free.

Many years later a customer we'll call Alec M. and I were on the fourteenth hole at Pebble Beach. Alec had a top of the line slice and there were multi-zillion dollar homes on the right side of the fourteenth fairway — homes with very big windows. One of Alec's slices was headed right for one of those windows. Inexplicably I shouted, "Whoever breaks it pays for it." From Alec: "What did you say?" Happily, my answer was carried away by the wind.

Working as a Caddy

Beginning in my early twenties, I became a people watcher. That means I actually SEE people when I look at them and I listen and respond carefully in a conversation. It's a very interesting avocation and also logical since humans are the only living creatures with whom I can communicate.

With that preface you can understand why it would be a no-brainer for me to caddy for a gentleman participating in the Pro-Am part of an important golf tournament held at the Riviera Country Club in Los Angeles. I'm thinking I could watch and perhaps even talk with professional golfers and other celebrities. Boy, was I naïve. The pros are working. When they do engage in conversation, it's with the celebs. Perfectly understandable.

My first time out, the celebrity was Tom Lasorda, then manager of the Los Angeles Dodgers. Tom obviously didn't play a lot of golf. On this one hole, he and I were quite a distance from the rest of the group. He took a mighty swing, moved the ball about thirty yards and said — loud enough for me to hear, "What the hell. I don't do this for a living." I couldn't resist saying good-naturedly, "Thank God for that Tom." He turned toward me and his look translated into "Who is this guy?"

The second year, the celebrity was Johnny Mathis. I believe the pro was Hale Irwin.

Mathis wasn't as bad as Lasorda but he hit a lot of wayward shots. On almost all those occasions Mathis' caddy would say, "Nice shot John."

Once again, big mouth couldn't resist. When I was close enough to the "nice shot" caddy I asked him if he played golf. He answered, "Yes" and I followed my first question with, "How good are you?" When he said he was a 2 handicap I responded, "Then you know good from bad on a golf course so what's with the 'Nice shot John' after he really dorks one?"

By then Mathis was close enough to hear my question and for the first time looked at me with a "Mind your manners" look. I knew then my question was rhetorical since it was obvious that John's caddy was more than JUST a caddy.

St. Andrews

When I'm playing, a caddy who knows the course and can engage in interesting conversation ends up having a good day financially.

One of my most memorable rounds took place on the legendary St. Andrews in Scotland. The gentleman on my bag that day was top of the line. I'll refer to him as John.

He pronounced my name as Fronk. Early on, my friends were giving me some good-natured heat regarding my multi-colored (madras) pants. From John, "Pay them no mind Fronk. It must be convenient to get out of bed and come to the course without changing clothes."

Later he told me of a man he was working for that was accompanied by his wife. As they approached the bridge not far from the 18th tee, John told this couple the age of that bridge. I believe it was about seven hundred years old. According to John the lady's response was "My goodness, how did they get the cars over it?"

John's final jewel of the day: He asked, "Do you know what happiness is Fronk?" After my quizzical look, "A long walk with the putter." I totally agreed.

Charles Hamm, Caddy Extraordinaire

When I was playing Pebble Beach a lot, my favorite caddy was Charles Hamm. He wasn't always available since he was suspended with some regularity.

Charles could be described as a free spirit who had almost zero comprehension of the effect of his words and actions. Charles and I were on the thirteenth tee at Pebble one beautiful day when one of the other players in our foursome asked Charles, "Is there any water on this hole?" He meant bodies of water between the tee and green.

Notwithstanding Charles' eccentricities, when I knew him he was a very bright person. I say that because I'm reasonably sure Charles was thinking 'Why is he asking me that question?' Thirteen is a hole where you see most of it from the tee and you can certainly see the landing area for every class of golfer. I wasn't surprised then when Charles answered, "Yes," and pointed to a drinking facility not far from the tee.

I believe Charles was suspended for telling a lady, who had to be totally without any sense of humor, a 'risqué' joke that she reported to the clubhouse. The joke, "Why did the mouse marry the elephant? Because he had to."

My favorite 'Charles' story: He was packing a double one cloudy day and as he and his unsuspecting customers approached the tenth green at Pebble Beach, a light rain had begun. I should point out that the tenth green is about as far as you can get from the clubhouse and still be on the golf course. After his players had finished putting, Charles walked up to them and said, "Could you please pay me now? I have a dinner engagement in Carmel." From the tenth green, Carmel is a fairly short walk on the beach.

To this day I don't know the reaction of Charles' clients. I do know he left.

$$\Omega$$